The Seven Core Principles
of Waldorf Education

Dec 6, 2017

Dearest Curt,

Thank you for all your
dedicated work for our school

Mystery Verse

Summer Solstice:
Receive the light

Fall Equinox:
Gaze into the World

Winter Solstice:
Shield against the Darkness

Spring Equinox:
know Thyself.

R. Steiner

Thank you,
Pedagogical Council

The Seven Core Principles
of
Waldorf Education

Elan Leibner, editor

Pedagogical Section Council of North America

Printed with support from the Waldorf Curriculum Fund

Printed by:

Waldorf Publications at the
Research Institute for Waldorf Education
38 Main Street
Chatham, NY 12037

Title: *The Seven Core Principles of Waldorf Education*
Editor: Elan Leibner
Layout: Ann Erwin
Proofreader: Melissa Merkling
Cover art: *Lifting the Veils,* painting by Ursula Stone
Silver Threads Collection, used with permission of the artist

ISBN: 978-1-943582-09-9

Table of Contents

Introduction

How and Why Did the Core Principles Come into Being?

THE GENESIS OF THE DOCUMENT at the heart of this book can be traced to the Kolisko Conference that took place at Rudolf Steiner College in Fair Oaks, CA. Keynote speaker Dr. Michaela Glöckler presented what she termed "The Five Core Values of Waldorf Education." Those were:

1. Child Development
2. Developmental Curriculum
3. Methodology (artistic metamorphosis)
4. Relationships
5. Spiritual Orientation

She drew those five on a five-pointed star, emphasizing that they were not hierarchical but rather interrelated: A study of one would lead to a question answered by the next. So, for example, once child development is studied, the question becomes: What would best support a child during each stage of development? Thus we arrive at the next core value: a developmental curriculum. I noted this schema and used it, with modifications and elaborations, over the following several years both in teacher preparation courses and in public lectures.

At the same time, there was an ongoing process between the Association of Waldorf Schools of North America (AWSNA) and the budding charter school movement regarding the use of the names "Waldorf" and "Rudolf Steiner," which are service marks owned by AWSNA. Since the Pedagogical Section is not a group made up of organizations, but rather of individuals, and since those individuals could be, and indeed were, members of both independent and charter schools, it seemed that the Pedagogical Section Council (PSC) might be able to act as an honest broker and facilitate some movement forward.

We approached the leadership of AWSNA and offered to write a document that could serve as a common point of departure for the conversation. The idea was that if both groups could accept it and say, "Yes, this is what we are trying to do," then the dialog could focus on how to do "it" better and on how each group could succeed and struggle with the execution of these intentions.

The idea was embraced, and the PSC set out to create such a document. We used Dr. Glöckler's template and elaborated it as the document that was finally presented to both AWSNA and the leadership of the Alliance for Public Waldorf Education in the spring of 2012. In a mediation meeting held in San Francisco, both groups endorsed the document.

The PSC saw itself as the guardian of the pedagogy, the impulse. We deliberately stayed away from the social and political questions at the heart of the debate between independent and public schools, not because they are not important, but because we chose to focus on the task of the teacher standing before students, in whatever context.

That is the historical context that led to the writing of the Core Principles document. Since it was first disseminated, the document has undergone periodic revisions based on comments and suggestions made by colleagues. (The most recent revision was made in 2014.) The PSC has never meant it to be "the final word" on what Waldorf education is.

Following the publication of the document, boards of trustees and faculties decided to study it. We began hearing from them that the wording was too cryptic, too dense. The PSC had deliberately kept the language as concise as possible, for the document was written with experienced educators in mind (those who were engaged in the AWSNA-Alliance process). New readers were not quite as seasoned, and the pithiness of the formulation became a problem. So we decided to write a series of articles in support of studying the document. The articles were written with the idea that the persons reading them were not already deeply familiar with anthroposophy and Waldorf education, but were sympathetic. We were not trying to justify Waldorf education to a skeptic, but to help a friend understand it better.

The essays were published in the *Research Bulletin for Waldorf Education* over several issues, and have now been collected, reviewed, augmented with a few new contributions, and prepared for publication in this book. We hope that this format makes both the document and the supporting articles useful to those who want to dive into the deep water that is Waldorf education.

– Elan Leibner
For the Pedagogical Section Council
March 2017

The Seven Core Principles
of Waldorf Education

CORE PRINCIPLE 1 *Image of the Human Being*
The human being in its essence is a being of Spirit, soul, and body. Childhood and adolescence, from birth to age 21, are the periods during which the Spirit/soul gradually takes hold of the physical instrument that is our body. The Self is the irreducible spiritual individuality within each one of us, which continues its human journey through successive incarnations.

CORE PRINCIPLE 2 *Phases of Child Development*
This process of embodiment has an archetypal sequence of approximately seven-year phases, and each child's development is an individual expression of the archetype. Each phase has unique and characteristic physical, emotional, and cognitive dimensions.

CORE PRINCIPLE 3 *Developmental Curriculum*
The curriculum is created to meet and support the phase of development of the individual and the class. From birth to age 7 the guiding principle is that of imitation; from 7 to 14 the guiding principle is that of following the teacher's guidance; during the high school years the guiding principle is idealism and the development of independent judgment.

CORE PRINCIPLE 4 *Freedom in Teaching*
Rudolf Steiner gave indications for the development of a new

pedagogical art, with the expectation that "the teacher must invent this art at every moment." Out of the understanding of child development and Waldorf pedagogy, the Waldorf teacher is expected to meet the needs of the children in the class out of his/her insights and the circumstances of the school. Interferences with the freedom of the teacher by the school, parents, standardized testing regimens, or the government, while they may be necessary in a specific circumstance (for safety or legal reasons, for example), are nonetheless compromises.[1]

CORE PRINCIPLE 5 *Methodology of Teaching*
There are a few key methodological guidelines for the grade school and high school teachers. Early childhood teachers work with these principles appropriate to the way in which the child before the age of 7 learns, out of imitation rather than direct instruction:

> » Artistic metamorphosis: The teacher should understand, internalize, and then present the topic in an artistic form.[2]
> » From experience to concept: The direction of the learning process should proceed from the students' soul activities of willing, through feeling to thinking. In the high school, the context of the experience is provided at the outset.[3]
> » Holistic process: proceeding from the whole to the parts and back again, and addressing the whole human being.
> » Use of rhythm and repetition.[4]

CORE PRINCIPLE 6 *Relationships*
Enduring human relationships between students and their teachers are essential and irreplaceable. The task of all teachers is to work with the developing individuality of each student and with each class as a whole. Truly human pedagogical relationships gain in depth and stability when they are cultivated over many

years. They cannot be replaced by instruction utilizing computers or other electronic means. Healthy working relationships with parents and colleagues are also essential to the well-being of the class community and the school.

CORE PRINCIPLE 7 *Spiritual Orientation*
In order to cultivate the imaginations, inspirations, and intuitions needed for their work, Rudolf Steiner gave the teachers an abundance of guidance for developing an inner, meditative life. This guidance includes individual professional meditations and an imagination of the circle of teachers forming an organ of spiritual perception. Faculty and individual study, artistic activity, and research form additional facets of ongoing professional development.

ENDNOTES
1   A note about school governance: While not directly a pedagogical matter, school governance can be an essential aspect of freedom in teaching. Just as a developmental curriculum should support the phases of child development, school governance should support the teachers' pedagogical freedom (while maintaining the school's responsibilities towards society).
2   The term "artistic" does not necessarily mean the traditional arts (singing, drawing, sculpting, etc.), but rather that, like those arts, the perceptually manifest reveals something invisible through utilizing perceptible media. Thus a math problem or science project can be just as artistic as storytelling or painting.
3   This mirrors the development of human cognition, which is at first active in the limbs and only later in the head.
4   There are four basic rhythms with which the Waldorf teacher works. The most basic of those is the day-night (or two-day) rhythm. Material that is presented on a given day is allowed to "go to sleep" before it is reviewed and brought to conceptual clarity on the following day. A second rhythm is that of the week. It is "the interest rhythm" and teachers strive to complete an engagement with a topic within a week of working on it. A paper

that is returned to the student after more than a week will no longer be interesting to the student. The only interesting thing will be the teacher's comments, but the topic itself is already past the "interest window." A third rhythm is that of four weeks. A block, or unit of instruction, is usually best covered in four-week periods. This life-rhythm can be understood in contemplation of feminine reproductive cycles, for example, and can be said to bring a topic to a temporary level of maturity. The last of the pedagogical rhythms is that of a year. This is the time it can take for a new concept to be mastered to the degree that it can be used as a capacity. Thus a mathematical concept introduced early in third grade should be mastered sufficiently to be assumed as a capacity for work at the beginning of fourth grade.

A Contribution to the Study of the First Core Principle

Elan Leibner

CORE PRINCIPLE **1** *Image of the Human Being*
The human being in its essence is a being of Spirit, soul, and body. Childhood and adolescence, from birth to age 21, are the periods during which the Spirit/soul gradually takes hold of the physical instrument that is our body. The Self is the irreducible spiritual individuality within each one of us, which continues its human journey through successive incarnations.

There are four thoughts woven together in the first Core Principle:

» The human being is a being of Spirit, soul, and body.
» The process of incarnating the Spirit and soul into the body takes approximately 21 years.
» The essential Self is an irreducible spiritual principle.
» The Self incarnates repeatedly and in human form.

Let us review these thoughts in order.

1. Rudolf Steiner's basic introduction to the nature of the human being is found in the first chapter of his foundational book *Theosophy*. The threefold (body, soul, spirit) principle is presented and then elaborated upon considerably. Briefly, and using Steiner's own example, when we look at a flower in the meadow, there are three aspects to consider: Our bodily senses give us the stimuli necessary for the flower to enter our

14

consciousness; our spirit allows us to recognize the flower as, for example, a daisy, which means recognizing a lawfulness that would remain even when the physical specimen is no longer before us; our soul forms a relationship between our subject and the flower in question.

The following exercise can help make the threefold human being more readily comprehensible: Place a manufactured object such as a pencil or a paper clip before you. Describe its appearance in detail (size, color, shape, smell, and any other pertinent sensory attribute). This description originates with what Steiner calls the bodily aspect of the human being.

Next, describe your personal response to this object: like or dislike, attraction or repulsion, and so forth. This response originates in what Steiner calls the soul.

Finally, try to articulate the concept of the object. In manufactured objects the concept is nearly identical with the function. A paper clip is meant to clip papers together, for example, and the clipping is more or less the thought or intention that brought it into being. You can try to follow as best you can the series of steps that led from the functional intention through the manufacturing process to the presence of the object before you. This thought process, which is not observable through the senses, originates in what Steiner calls the spirit. Only the spirit can perceive the spiritual, hidden aspects of the world around us.

2. The process of incarnating (literally "entering the flesh") takes 21 years on average. In their discussions of the second Core Principle, Holly Koteen-Soulé and Adam Blanning present the phases of this process in detail. A good source for this idea is Steiner's book *The Education of the Child in the Light of Spiritual Science*.

From a pedagogical perspective, one of the most succinct articulations of the relationship between spirit and soul, on the one hand, and the body, on the other, can be found in the first lecture of *Foundations of Human Experience/Study of Man*. This lecture cannot be recommended highly enough for anyone who wants the quintessence of Waldorf education brought in an astonishingly concise formulation. Steiner presents in few words a whole cosmic drama in which the individuality of the child comes into the world and needs the teacher's help in order to learn how to function properly in the flesh, so to speak.

3. An essential idea in Steiner's presentation of human nature is that the spiritual core of the human being is not a reducible epiphenomenon of matter, but rather that it predates and also survives physical existence. This notion is presented in detail in the second chapter of *Theosophy* and throughout many of Steiner's writings. (We elected to capitalize Spirit in the first Core Principle in order to emphasize its eternal aspect.) In the first lecture of *Study of Man,* Steiner emphasizes that the existence of the spirit before birth is just as crucial an aspect of the human condition as the much more commonly held idea of immortality as referring only to life after death. Talents, challenges, social circumstances, and many other seemingly random dimensions of life assume meaning and significance of a whole different magnitude when seen in the light of reincarnation, or even just contemplated by that light. For the teacher, the tasks implicit in Core Principles 6 and 7 are substantially affected by the notion of repeated earth lives.

4. Further regarding the human being's journey through successive incarnations: In anthroposophy a human being was, is, and will be a human being. In other traditions, the various

kingdoms of nature are considered interchangeable for purposes of reincarnation. Steiner considered this view erroneous, and in the chapter on reincarnation mentioned earlier (in the book *Theosophy*), he explains that repeated earth lives can be thought of in a similar manner to waking up one morning with the results of the previous day's actions and plans. Just as it would not make sense to wake up as a sparrow tomorrow morning, so it would not be true to consider a human being as having been either a blade of grass or a grasshopper during a previous life on earth. Precisely because we are beings capable of new beginnings, new creations, we must live with the consequences of our actions and inactions (and even, according to Steiner, our thoughts and feelings) over time, both from day to day and from one life to the next.

Now that the four basic thoughts of the first Core Principle have been introduced, let us consider them in more detail. For Rudolf Steiner, the human being stands uniquely positioned between the spiritual world and the physical world. Human beings are the only earthly beings with the capacity to originate, to create new beginnings out of spiritual insights, and the only spiritual beings with the physical tools to work right into earthly substance.

To put it succinctly: Chimps can't write poetry; angels can't plant corn. There is no way to account for human spiritual activity from a purely material-causality perspective: It makes no sense to say, for instance, of the work of William Shakespeare that on Sunday night the weather was bad, but the stew his wife made for dinner was very good and his daughter slept well, and so therefore The Bard woke up the next day and wrote Hamlet's famous soliloquy. One can investigate the material and emotional events preceding the creation of a great work of art, but one cannot say that those circumstances caused the art to be created. Something surprising and uniquely individual transpires in every new creation, something that points to a level of existence at which every human being is a complete species unto him- or herself. We can predict with relative certainty what a weather pattern or a particular diet will do to my dog, but we cannot predict what painting my wife will create because of the weather outside and the meal she just ate. To the extent that we eat, breathe, walk, and so on, we are a species like other mammal species; to the extent that we create new beginnings, we are each a species unto ourselves. Even persons who are not particularly creative create something new in the form of their biography, and this makes them unique in a way that no animal ever is.

At the opposite end of the body-spirit polarity, human beings are uniquely able among spiritual beings to work directly into material existence. We can conceive an idea, e.g., building a new school somewhere, and then go about realizing that idea in the physical world. In the example of Hamlet's soliloquy, Shakespeare could take pen to paper and bring the words he conceived into a form accessible to other people. Other spiritual beings require the assistance of human beings if their intentions are to be made manifest on earth.

The soul in Steiner's tripartite image of the human being occupies a middle ground between spirit and body. I can see the daisy with my physical senses (by means of my body) and learn to recognize more and more what makes it a daisy (by what we have termed spirit), but the soul forms a personal relationship of liking or disliking, caring about or choosing to ignore that which I encounter. If the sensory aspect constitutes the fleeting materialization of the daisy, and the concept "daisy" is the eternal, universal thought, the relationship my soul forms with the daisy makes for a uniquely personal relationship between the daisy and me. It tells something about me, rather than about the daisy.

For Steiner, every human being is a spirit living temporarily in a physical body, and the soul is the mediator between the two. The soul gathers impressions of the physical world through the bodily senses and brings those impressions for the spirit to gain knowledge and wisdom, and then it brings the impulses of the spirit into manifestation on earth through the activation of the will. The 21-year period at the beginning of life is, according to Steiner, the time it takes for the spirit to reach earth maturity to the point of being fully capable of leading its own life. In many states this age used to be the voting age, and in many it is still a marker for various aspects of adult consent.

Waldorf education is not the only pedagogical approach that begins with a view of the human being. It is, in fact, important to realize that every educational system begins with such a view, whether explicit or not. This view covers such questions as the essential nature of being human (e.g., the result of a series of cellular and molecular accidents; a being created by God on the sixth of seven days, and so forth). The pedagogy would then consider the development from childhood to adulthood and what a successful human being, and therefore a successful educational process, "looks like." If you believe that a human being is a complicated animal, that the animal is finally only compounded of material particles, that childhood is merely a stage of being a small adult, that success is measurable through some yardstick extrinsic to the individual (e.g., economic or academic achievement), then you will also design an educational system that aims to achieve goals that are measured outside of the individual that is being educated. In similar fashion, if you believe that all human beings are born in sin, that the goal of life is to avoid hell and join God and the saints in Heaven, and that the Church is the only door to the rightful path, then you will design a schooling that will bring the young person into the folds of the Mother Church, and this will then guide the choice of content and methods. I mention this since looking back on one's education and discerning its philosophical underpinnings can be an enlightening exercise.

If, in contrast, you hold the view that the essential nature of every student is an eternal, spiritual individuality that has to fashion its own journey in freedom, then your pedagogy will endeavor to support that spiritual element in developing and achieving its own aims. The skills and capacities that you will strive to nurture within the student will not be ends in themselves, nor will they be preparations for predetermined later stages, but rather vehicles for the student's "I" to find its way in the world. The idea that education is an attempt to reconnect a human being with his or her own goals, and that these goals are uniquely individual, finding their place in a context of relationships and activity—this idea would then rightfully become a crucial principle of your pedagogy. It is neatly summed in the oft-quoted edict: "Our highest endeavor must be to develop free human beings who are able of themselves to impart purpose and meaning to their lives."[1]

ENDNOTE

1   From the foreword by Marie Steiner to Rudolf Steiner's Ilkley lecture cycle, published in English as *A Modern Art of Education*. Forest Row, UK: Rudolf Steiner Press, 1972, p.23.

REFERENCES

Rudolf Steiner. *The Education of the Child in the Light of Spiritual Science*. Forest Row, UK: Rudolf Steiner Press, 1965.

_____. *Theosophy*. Great Barrington, MA: Anthroposophic Press, 1994.

_____. *Study of Man*. Forest Row, UK: Rudolf Steiner Press, 2007.

Two Contributions to the Study of the Second Core Principle

CORE PRINCIPLE 2 *Phases of Child Development*
This process of embodiment has an archetypal sequence of approximately seven-year phases, and each child's development is an individual expression of the archetype. Each phase has unique and characteristic physical, emotional, and cognitive dimensions.

First Contribution

Holly Koteen-Soulé

What makes the four-year-old different from the ten-year-old, and what makes them both different from the seventeen-year-old? The Second Core Principle of Waldorf education recognizes the critical importance of understanding the universal patterns of child development from birth to age 21, as well as the distinct characteristics of the first, second, and third seven-year cycles in the life of the child and adolescent.

To understand the differences, we need to refer to the fourfold human being as described by Rudolf Steiner. The fourfold human being is comprised of the physical body, the etheric body, the astral body, and the "I"-organization. Although Steiner uses the word *body* in relation to the etheric and astral, he notes that these are actually "bodies" of forces, rather than material substances.[1]

Each of the first three bodies is connected with one of the seven-year periods of development and lends to that period and the developing child certain characteristic attributes.

Birth to Age 7

The physical body is born at the emergence of the baby from the womb and is preeminent during the child's first seven years of growth and development. Just as the child's physical body is emancipated from the womb of the mother, according to Steiner, the other bodies also have a birth or emancipation from their protective sheaths.[2] The subsequent births of the finer bodies are as important for Waldorf education as the child's physical birth.

From birth to around the age of 7, young children are working on and out of their physical natures. Sensory experiences and movement are the means by which they develop their physical capacities and explore the world. Endowed with immense will forces, they take in the world by active doing. Whatever they sense in their surrounding, they become and act out or imitate. They master the essential human capacities of walking, speaking, and thinking through imitating the adults in their environment. They think through doing and learn by imitation.

The etheric body works in conjunction with the physical body during these first seven years, bringing forming forces to the physical body and maintaining its organic life processes. Edmond Schoorel suggests that the etheric body has its "inner birth" at the time the physical body goes through its "outer birth," in that the baby is able to maintain its own life processes separate from its mother.[3] Approximately seven years later, when the child's physical growth and development has reached a certain conclusion and fewer etheric forces are needed to form and maintain the physical body, the etheric body is born or emancipated from the physical body. A portion of the etheric forces is freed for new adventures.

The eruption of the child's permanent teeth can be seen as a sign of the conclusion of this first phase of development.

Between 7 and 14

With the birth of the etheric body, some of the child's formative life forces are now available for psychological rather than physiological activities—for instance, for the forming of concepts, memories, habits, and temperament. The physical body is still active in gathering sensory experiences, but now the child of this age can form and recall inner pictures of his or her own experiences. This allows the child to be ready for direct instruction and to receive guidance from the teacher as a beloved source of worldly knowledge and skills. During the first seven years, rhythm is brought to the life of the young child out of regular and repetitive rituals in his or her surroundings, as well as out of the etheric forces of the parent and early childhood teacher. In the second period, rhythm and repetition help grade school children begin to strengthen their own etheric bodies and habit life.

Experiences connected to lively pictures and a rich palette of feelings are the ones most readily received and recalled. During the first seven years, the feeling life was still under the sway of the bodily instincts, impulses, and desires. Now the yet "unborn" astral body is connecting with the newly-freed etheric forces, and the feeling life is slowly awakening. Feelings can be strong, even extreme, and often come over the child like uncontrollable weather. The inner life of the teacher, along with her stories and artistic activities, nourishes and brings order, sense, and consequence to the imagination and developing inner life of the child between 7 and 14.

Whereas the young child thinks by doing, the grade school child thinks through images and pictures. This is not yet the abstract thinking capacity that will develop later, but rather a sense for wholeness, for relationships, and for the deeper meaning of things that can arise from a well-developed feeling life and artistic practice.

Between 14 and 21

The outer birth of the astral body is heralded physically by the onset of puberty and the beginning of adolescence. The physical changes that signify the beginning of this period are readily recognizable. Was there also an "inner birth" of the astral body, as there was with the etheric body, and if so when did that occur? The moment when the young child, around the age of 2 or 3 years, begins to say "I" signals, according to Schoorel, the "inner birth" of the astral body.[4]

As an early childhood teacher, this awareness helped me greatly to understand the changes that I perceived in young children as they began to refer to themselves as an "I." This event in the life of a young child signals the end of a unitary consciousness or oneness with everything and a beginning of the separation that is required for the human being to be reflective and to think. The interval between the inner and outer birth of the astral body is around ten or eleven years. The seed of self-consciousness and abstract thinking that is planted at three takes many years—indeed the whole of the development between 7 and 14—before it is ready to flower.

Rudolf Steiner speaks about this in his seminal talk on education, *The Education of the Child in the Light of Spiritual Science*. In this lecture he says,

> Thought must take hold in a living way in the
> children's minds so that they first learn and then judge.
> What the intellect has to say about any matter should
> be said only when all the other faculties have spoken.

Before then the intellect has only an intermediary part to play; its task is to comprehend what occurs and what is experienced in feeling, to receive it exactly as it is, not letting unripened judgment immediately come in and take over.[5]

During the final period of child development, the intellect and abstract thinking capacities come at last to the foreground. With the astral body emancipated from its protective sheath, the search for truth and a sense of self begin. The young person who is searching for his or her own truth cannot help but question the authority of adults and teachers. Reverence for the experience of one's elders is quickly replaced with criticalness. This is the expression of strengthening intellectual capacities, which is already present to some degree between 12 and 14.

These three periods of child development are sometimes referred to as the eras of will, of feeling, and of thinking. However, the beginning of each seven-year period is more strongly influenced by the will element, the middle by the feeling element, and the final third of each period by the thinking element. It is as if there is an echoing of the past development and foreshadowing of the future development in each period. *Pars pro toto:* In each part the whole is reflected.

Whereas the early years of adolescence are often marked by rebellion and dissolution, as young teenagers seek to find their own way and to develop their ability to think and make well-founded judgments, idealism and excitement about possibilities that lie ahead characterize the latter years of the period from 14 to 21.

Archetypes and Not Norms

These developmental archetypes help us understand what we are observing in our students and inform the shaping and presenting of our lessons. The timing of developmental changes can vary widely among normally developing children, as can the individual means by which they express the changes that are taking place during a particular period of growth and maturation. Our knowledge of the archetypes should not blind us to seeing our individual students.

The Birth of the "I"

Around the age of 21, the fourth birth—the birth of the ego or "I"—takes place, crowning the journey of child development and giving the young adult the means by which to direct his or her own life path and further development. For Schoorel, the inner birth of the "I" occurs at what is sometimes called the nine-year change.[6] This represents a distinct shift during the second period of child development when—like the milestone of early childhood at age 3—the child experiences both the pain of separation and the enthusiasm for a newly-found independence.

The Higher Bodies as Teachers

Waldorf teachers are familiar with the advice given by Steiner that is often called "The Pedagogical Law."[7] Schoorel indicates that the sequential births of the four bodies are the physiological basis for this principle.[8] In the process of development from birth to 21, the unborn members of the human constitution influence the development of the lower members, the next higher member having the strongest influence. The higher body, as yet unborn, works on the lower body that has been born already. Specifically, the unborn ether body, with the help of the environment, educates the physical body; the unborn astral body educates the ether body, and the unborn "I" educates the astral body. In each case, this occurs with the help of the environment, which includes parents and teachers.

This education is not, however, a one-way process. Schoorel speaks about the relation between the etheric and physical bodies during the period between birth and age 7 in this way:

> The stronger the imprint that the ether body makes on the physical body, the more the ether body itself will change and the more easily it will liberate itself from the physical body.[9]

It makes sense that this principle would also hold true for the relation between the astral and the ether during the second seven-year cycle and between the astral and the "I" during the third period.

For me, the recognition of the origin of "The Pedagogical Law" and its physiological basis is tremendously helpful in understanding more deeply the process of development during the first 21 years and the distinct characteristics of the three seven-year cycles. It also gives me a new picture of my role as a helper of the child's own unborn members. Lastly, it underscores for me that the goal of our work is to support young human beings in their process of achieving self-determining independence.

ENDNOTES

1   Rudolf Steiner. *The Education of the Child in the Light of Spiritual Science*. Forest Row, UK: Rudolf Steiner Press, 1965, pp.9–16. Steiner uses the German word *Leib* rather than *Körper*, both of which mean "body" in English. *Körper* is a cognate of a more physical organization (akin to the English "corpus" or even "corpse"), whereas *Leib*, as its sound suggests, is more akin to a living body. "A body of knowledge" is an example of how "body" can have a meaning closer to *Leib* than to *Körper*.
2   Ibid., pp.21–22.
3   Edmond Schoorel. *The First Seven Years: Physiology of Childhood*. Fair Oaks, CA: Rudolf Steiner College Press, p.25.
4   Ibid, p.26.
5   Op. cit., Steiner, p.26.

6   Op. cit., Schoorel, p.27.
7   Rudolf Steiner. *Curative Education*, lecture 2. Forest Row, UK: Rudolf Steiner Press, 1972.
8   Ibid., p.24.
9   Ibid., p.22.

Second Contribution
The Breathing Rhythms of Childhood Biography
Adam Blanning, MD

Outer experiences are most powerful when they resonate within. As human beings we are deeply influenced by those encounters which speak to a truth we already carry in our own inner world. We appreciate things much more deeply when we can live into both their inner and outer manifestations—a love song sounds so beautiful and inspiring when we are in love, a heartbreak song unsettlingly insightful even if you have heard the song a hundred times before. We do not, however, learn to love by listening to love songs. The capacity for loving develops first. We are sometimes fooled that things happen the other way around and told that we are really defined and shaped by the information given to us. Most of the world relies on that dynamic, as it seeks to flood us with information as though we were each a large vessel that will be shaped by the sweet wine poured in. We are all swayed by these outer prods and recommendations, but that is not the main developmental dynamic of human growth.

There is an antidote to this outer tide. It comes whenever our inner world makes an unprompted shift. Unprompted, that is, because it does not arise as a reaction to something from the outside. Instead of information coming to us from the outside and prompting us to react in either a positive or a negative way, the new experience starts deep within and then gradually pushes its way out. It brings with it a strong need to re-evaluate all that is around us: We see things in a new way. This can feel disconcerting because particularly in adult biography it may feel as though there are no outer circumstances or changes asking for a change; all may be relatively stable in terms of relationships, work, home, and hobbies. But in spite of there being no outer logic we meet an inner "itchiness" that forces us to grow and reorient—convenient or not.

These inner-to-outer shifts follow a strong seven-year rhythm. Some of the earlier shifts are accompanied by prominent changes in outer growth, such as the appearance of adult teeth at age 6 to 7 or the pubertal changes that lead up to the fourteenth year. Even when children are not physically changing in dramatic ways, their inner world is rarely still. The inner life of a child is never truly stagnant; the child hardly has a chance to come to rest because every few years a new aspect of consciousness is being "birthed." As teachers and parents we should seek to know and to anticipate the rhythms of these inner changes. For then they can be supported and met, acknowledged with encouraging experiences of interaction, adventure, and curriculum. Like hearing a love song when you are first falling in love, when this "resonating" happens, the child is reassured that the world is a good place. Such striving to meet and encourage children as they blossom into new capacity stands at the very heart of Waldorf education and its curriculum.

The rotating rhythms of childhood biography unfold through the differentiated activity of the four members of the human being. Each time a child begins to see the world with new eyes, he or she is linked to a new capacity for experiencing oneself. These new capacities come from many small "births," not just the main one we think of at the end of pregnancy. They relate not only to the physical body, but also to the new and differentiated activities of the etheric body, astral body and "I." Each of these members is present at birth, but proceeds to make significant steps in independent activity and conscious capacity over the first twenty-one years of life.

The progression of these multiple births is very helpfully laid out by Dr. Edmond Schoorel in his book, *The First Seven Years: Physiology of Childhood.*[1] He describes how the development of each member needs to be described from two different aspects: first, in terms of how its activity becomes individualized (relating to an activity within the body, an "inner birth"), which is later followed by a further step through which those same forces become independent from the body and move into more conscious activity (an "outer birth," very much analogous to moving from a stage of *building* organs to now using the organs).

From Dr. Schoorel's description we can understand that the **physical body** becomes *individualized* with the process of conception when a distinct physical structure is formed, a fertilized egg which within hours becomes a cluster of cells that grows into an embryo. Then about nine months later, the physical body becomes *independent* through the birthing process when it physically separates from the mother's body. Conception gives a physical anchoring, a physically-perceptible hereditary basis for growth; then birth gives independent physical existence.

Parallel steps of maturation can also be traced for the etheric, astral, and "I":

» The shifts for the **etheric body** are: first, the physical *birth process*, in which the etheric body becomes individualized and distinct from the mother's etheric forces; and then the *seventh year* of life, when etheric forces are emancipated from their earlier task of growth and organ development and are now freed for activities of abstract thought and memory.

» For the **astral body**: the first birth comes in the *third year* (age 2–3, "the terrible twos,") when astral sensing and the emotional life awaken in a new way through the forces of sympathy and antipathy; then outwardly through *adolescence* (age 12–14), accompanied by physical changes of sexual maturation, when the feeling life opens to experience social cohesion and isolation, joy and sorrow, and artistic depth and sensitivity.

» For the **"I"-being**: the first birth comes in the *ninth year* (often referred to as the "Rubicon"), when there is a strong realization of individual identity and a separateness from parents, teachers, siblings, and friends; and then again in the *twenty-first year*, when experiences of true individual intention and morality dawn, often accompanied by a major step out into independent adult life, away from the family and community of origin.

We will now take these nodal points (conception, birth, 3rd year, 7th year, 9th year, 14th year, 21st year) and explore how the changing activity of the corresponding spiritual member relates to aspects of growth and awareness. We will begin with the processes of conception and birth, as the dynamics of these processes can have an important influence on a child's later experience.

Conception: With this step the physical body becomes distinct from the body of the mother and father, the very first step of individualization. Here begins the meeting of the hereditary stream (the physical body) and spiritual stream (the "I" and the astral body). All of the spiritual planning which has preceded this incarnation must now begin to reconcile itself to the physical

31

body. The way in which the physical meeting of egg and sperm happens (the combining of two hereditary streams) can influence how accessible the hereditary body becomes for the incarnating individuality. For the physical body, really a model body that must be penetrated and transformed, needs to be developmentally broken in for a child to make good use of it and to feel at home. If the body somehow remains inaccessible, it may impede entry into some aspects of life. As parents now often wait longer to have children and as fertilization processes can be manipulated in sophisticated ways it is worth considering this first "birthing" process and the dynamics involved.

Mechanically-facilitated conception processes, such as in-vitro fertilization or artificial insemination, remove the egg and sperm from the etheric sheaths of the mother's body which may exaggerate the density and gravity of the hereditary body. Also, older ova or sperm are known to increase the risk of birth defects and developmental challenges such as autism which we can similarly relate to an inherently dense physicality (and relatively weakened etheric) which limits or slows the healthy transformation of the physical body. Activities that support and stimulate the transformation of the hereditary body—such as sustained work, movement that makes the child red-faced and sweaty, dressing in layers to protect a child's warmth, giving a child the space and time to really work through a fever or inflammation as well as approaching deeds and tasks with real enthusiasm—all allow a child to find the right pathway for meeting and changing this physical body.

It is very important that looking at the process of conception does not lead to any kind of judgment or quiet condemnation of a conception process. That has a cooling effect on our relationship to a child. We should not second-guess a child's pathway in coming into the world. The priorities and dynamics at play are a wonder.[2] But looking at this first individualization of the physical body can help us know what experiences might particularly nourish the child in later life.

Birth and Infancy: With the birth that comes at the end of pregnancy two different "births" actually happen: The physical body becomes independent (its second birth), while etheric forces are individualized (a first etheric birth).

The step of physical independence is quite clear. The first breath, followed by the cutting of the umbilical cord, mark major steps of physical separation from the mother. A child now suddenly has to breathe on her own, produce her own warmth, suck, swallow, pee and poop. All of this was previously done by the placenta as part of the mother's body. Nutrition is admittedly not yet fully independent. A child needs breast milk and will not be able to truly nourish itself with food until quite some months later, but the specific physical bond to the mother has changed. Nutrition, as milk, does need to come to the child, but with this step of physical independence, the milk could come from a different mother or from formula. Nutrition is no longer linked specifically to the birth mother. This is an expression of the physical independence which was not possible during the pregnancy.

Etheric forces also become individualized with birth. The child now has her own etheric forces, evidenced by the way that a child can move to another family or be adopted into a whole new set of conditions. She will carry these etheric forces with her for the rest of her life. This does not mean that the etheric forces of the mother or a new caretaker do not have an influence— the etheric forces of surrounding adults are indeed exceptionally important. The child will need to bathe in them for the next seven years. Parents' etheric forces buffer the child and offer formative activity to the child's physical body. By being bathed in the parents' etheric protective harbor, children up to the age of 7 are able to live in a very imitative place, nourished by the rhythms, patterns and experiences brought by those who care for them.

The timing of this shift at the end of pregnancy is important for both the physical and etheric bodies, for the healthiest window for delivery comes when there has been enough growth that an infant can successfully switch from growing organs to using them. When a child is born quite early, parts of the body are required to abruptly become more physicalized. Organs which should still be in a developmental stage are forced into functional use. This earlier-than-ideal transition accentuates a shift away from body-directed, unconscious etheric growth activity (think of building the eyes, versus now needing to use the eyes to see). The resulting prematurely physicalized organs may fall into a hardened state, which may make it more difficult to really penetrate and claim the organs completely later on. Prematurity may accentuate the physicality of early life.

Prematurity may also significantly impact the etheric body as physical independence comes before etheric forces are really ready to be fully individualized. This can result in an overall etheric depletion. That depletion is compounded by the required shift in etheric activity toward wakeful, sensing activity. We can therefore view prematurity as a kind of karmic, situational acceleration of etheric forces from growth to wakefulness. This makes protection of the child's sensory life in the following years particularly important.

The transition from **infancy to toddlerhood** is marked by ever greater steps of physical strength and mobility, steps of self-contentment and steps of more independent nutrition, all related to a consolidation of the etheric forces that became independent

34

at birth. Outwardly a child makes many physical strides: learning to sit independently (6 months), crawl (9 months), stand (12 months), then walk, and eventually run. Through a reciprocal inward gesture, sensing connection to the body grows through the pathways of touch, balance, and self-movement. Capacities for more independent calming and self-soothing are also an important part of these years, connected to a greater sense of one's own well-being. Digestion and nutrition also improve. Many of these steps act in concert as evidenced by the fact that the transition from nursing as the major means for nutrition to the growth of teeth, to an interest in food, to the eventual ability to take in all types of food, follows much the same pathway as the capacity to calm oneself—whether it is learning to fall asleep without nursing, to recovering from the surprise of a fall, to learning to sleep in one's own bed, to restfully going back to sleep after a middle-of-the-night awakening. The child is learning to move the body, to feel the body, to be at home in the body.

Age 2–3 years: feeling and voicing a new experience of self. The third year of life marks another, big step on the pathway toward self-sensing as the astral body becomes individualized. Awareness of self comes to the fore in a new way because the astral body comes into new activity, with the possibility for sensing self and not-self. Sympathy and antipathy rush in, though still largely on a non-volitional level. These forces, which work now in the metabolism, will be later liberated into conscious awareness (at puberty). The "terrible twos" can be recognized as a kind of little "adolescence" and may bring forward a variety of excessively astral, cramp-like experiences and behaviors, such as: temper tantrums, breath-holding spells; aggressive behaviors such as hitting, biting, yelling, mood swings, and newfound likes and dislikes.

These burgeoning forces of awareness are inevitably a little scary—for the shift in experience happens first, rises into the feeling life, and only through time and repeated experience starts to feel normal. In that in-between space, there often arises a very real wish to go back, to return to when things were known and safe. Regressive behaviors—such as having trouble falling asleep, or simultaneously pushing for independence while having inexplicable separation anxiety, are part of that process. Children at this age need to find space to healthily explore and express these emotions. Parents/caretakers need to not fall into the trap of aggressively shutting down this new life (by repeatedly scolding), yet not be fooled into thinking that this astral bubbling is the expression of a deep and varied feeling life (i.e., when a child says she does not want to wear a coat when it is cold outside, this is not a reasoned response, much more an exercise in antipathy). Good rhythms help a child settle these swinging astral forces into their own physiology, so that they can learn to feel: Now it is time for eating, now for play, now for rest. Astral activity in the metabolism lends the possibility for this kind of rhythmic physiology.

The **kindergarten years** (3–5) serve as a time of consolidation for these astral forces in the child's limbs and metabolism. Children now seek and enjoy more active, cooperative play and activity. The astral forces that were so unsettled between two and three years now support a more robust metabolism, with the possibility to really use the body more and more capably. Stories settle very deeply into the child, as does festival life, with ever greater awareness that outer tales have inner truthfulness—i.e., that a child can successfully embody such qualities and deeds. Awareness of this maturation process comes as well, with the child's realizing that there is a difference in age, that an almost six-year-old is "bigger and stronger" than a four- or five-year-old.

Age 6–7 years: observing and remembering the world in a new way. At age 6½ to 7 years, etheric forces begin to be freed from their task of growth and organ formation. A portion of the etheric body now becomes independent, with forces available for new kinds of thinking and memory activity. New capacities for abstract thought come forward. Examples of this include the ability to understand jokes and puns—where very concrete thinking becomes more mobile. Up until this age, a child may imitate the pattern of a joke (such as a "knock-knock" joke), simply by repeating the progression, then inserting some new word(s) at the end, then knowing that it is time to laugh. With the liberated etheric, the sounds of a word can now move flexibly in consciousness so that it is possible to move back and forth between different meanings (e.g., "lettuce" and "let us"). This shift happens gradually, though it is not uncommon for a child to suddenly understand reading, when the capacity to understand abstract representations (letters) and their associated sounds becomes comprehensible.

This shift brings physical shifts as well, namely the first loss of baby teeth and the eruption of adult teeth. The proportions of the body also start to change—the head now relatively smaller as the limbs begin to grow at a faster rate.

This emancipation of etheric forces also influences the way a child interacts with the outside world. In many ways forces of growth and thought truly become the child's own—he is less imitative. A child may hear full well what is said, but is less easily shepherded. The root experience of being physiologically connected to parents and caretakers, especially to the mother, also fades.

Access to these liberated etheric forces of thought and memory becomes easier and more practiced in the eighth year. This brings new possibilities for attention.

Nine-year change: feeling oneself as different. With nine years, the "I" becomes individualized. This is characterized by a strong experience of individuality, of truly being a single person, separate from parents, teachers, and siblings.[3] Superficially, it could seem like this is a repeat of the seven-year change, in that a significant step of independence is achieved; but this experience of self is really happening on a different level and has a distinct character. We can perhaps best capture the seven-year change as a child experiencing for the first time a capacity for comfortably functioning away from parents; the seven-year-old child learns to be comfortable and successful as a *child among peers*. Children after the seven-year change are no longer dependent on the adults around them the way that a young child is. They can be carried by the tides of activity that carry a whole class—not necessarily so imitative of the teacher as united with their peers.

The nine-year change, in contrast, brings the experience of individual self: "I am my own person, I am a unique individuality" (and different from all my peers). I am different, not only from my parents, but from all other human beings. There is something unique about my experience. Children at this age start to realize the unique qualities (and also struggles and failings) of teachers, parents, and other caregivers who, up until this point, have been viewed with much broader admiration and a certain amount of blind acceptance. The darker aspects of individuality come more to the fore, along with the need to start finding an inner moral compass. Right and wrong can be felt inwardly in a new way— joys and challenges as well. Stronger friendships, based more strongly on individual qualities and interests, emerge.

This step of individualization of the "I" is felt primarily as an inward experience. This is more a change of experience of self than a shifting experience of how one sees the outside world. Worries often come at this age, not so much because of outer awakening but from new inner perception. Fears of death, of separation, and of possible loss often arise.

The nine-year change is an interesting threshold, because at a certain level, a child's comfort in the world becomes more directly dependent on her own inner resiliency and flexibility. For issues such as anxiety, or restlessness that results in continual disruptions and reassurance, the child must take an inner step. Up until this point it has been possible to work hard to shelter an anxious child from any outer experiences that could be worrisome or troubling. A child can still be carried and buffered by parents (especially to age 7). Between seven and nine those needs for extra reassurance or redirection can still generally be met—by the broader interest and activity of the class as a whole (who generally accept such behaviors without special consideration), and by some extra attention from the teacher or teacher's assistant. But with the step of "I"-individualization, children begin to notice things. Classmates may become less tolerant. And with the child's new awareness of self, there is no way to completely shield a child from experiencing isolation or loneliness.

There is a characteristic melancholy that often accompanies the nine-year change, but moving away from connection and dependence on the outside world can also be tremendously encouraging for the child. Now there can be the beginning of a new orientation, oriented toward one's own destiny and future tasks in the world. Enthusiasm and encouragement go a long way toward meeting and welcoming this first expression of true individuality. For when the nine-year change finds healthy expression, it provides an anchor for puberty and the adolescent years that follow.

Adolescence, 12–14 years: seeing and connecting to the outside world in new ways. With the liberation of astral forces into consciousness, sympathy and antipathy now move toward the outside world. They are still busy accomplishing last steps of growth in the body, as evidenced by the physical changes of sexual maturation (breast development, widening of hips for girls, widening of shoulders for boys, voice change), and adult patterns of hair growth (pubic, underarm, and facial hair). These mark some of the final orchestrations of physical growth by the astral body. As the astral body lives in opposites and contrasts—in light and dark, in sympathy and antipathy, in male and female—it is appropriate that at this stage bodies become more differentiated. The beginning of the menstrual cycles (menarche) marks an important shift, where astral forces begin to move rhythmically from physiology to consciousness, from an up-building, inward phase to a breaking-down, releasing phase. These changes come more quickly for girls than for boys, with an accompanying earlier release of these astral forces into the feeling life and into consciousness. For both boys and girls, shifting into a more adult awareness happens most healthily when it comes as a certain physiologic "ripeness" liberates forces from their activity in the body.

Astral forces can, of course, be prematurely pulled out, just as etheric forces can be prematurely pulled out through an early push for intellectualization. In both situations the child is asked to understand and participate in something which has not yet been properly birthed. Early pushes toward adult dress, media, and sexuality lead to an uneasy reliance on imitation—like a child who is trying to understand the humor of a pun before etheric forces for abstract thought have been fully liberated. So too the challenges of entering adolescence, with its shifting experiences, when this particular threshold has become so confused.

The astral shifting that defines adolescence has become more complicated as the physical, emotional, and social aspects of this change become less cohesive. It is increasingly common for the physical changes of sexual maturation to come at an earlier age (as early as 9), while true astral emotional and social maturation commonly come later. In earlier times, when the astral, "group" soul aspect of social life and community was much more dominant, pubertal changes marked a true transition into adult life and readiness for marriage and childbearing. With the current developmental emphasis on individualization, there is less predictability, though anecdotal observations suggest that Waldorf education may help allow astral forces to really complete their work in the body, with an accompanying delay in menarche.[4] Then the transition into adolescence can be more comfortable and cohesive.

Adolescence generally is a time of loosening, then reforming. Metabolic activities become more autonomous and separate from the models and patterns of the adults around them—the proverbial rush of hormones—though the free swings of astral activity go far beyond mood or sexuality. Instinctive knowledge about when to sleep, when to eat, what activities to prioritize, what feels boring, what is overstimulating, all gets lost for a period of time. These patterns lose their previous consistency because the astral forces that regulated them have appropriately become independent from the adults around them. A certain chaos ensues because the child must now learn how to guide his or her own physiology.

Social connection becomes paramount. Peer pressure gives form and influence to astral forces. It is now possible to be more deeply connected to friends, and alternatively more severely isolated from them, than at any previous time. Styles emerge, causes, passions, and a new artistic sensibility. In adolescence, a child can be inspired to a pursuit of true excellence, or apathetically find no inspiration for joining the adult world. The need to strongly influence this dysregulated inner world tempts many adolescents to self-medicate uncomfortable sensations away, which is accomplished by manipulating one's own astral forces. This can be done through sensory-seeking behaviors (extreme sports, video games, etc.) and/or substance-seeking behaviors (caffeine, nicotine, alcohol, drugs). It can also be accomplished by manipulating physiologic connections to our feeling life: through food (with patterns such as anorexia, bulimia, or binge-eating), by finding physical markers and re-enforcements of boundary (tattoos, cutting), through sexuality (where physical affection/encounter may seek to remedy emotional trauma or vulnerability).

As a teenager makes his way through adolescence, these liberated astral forces become more comfortable. The swings of emotion and connection are less volatile, the body a better known partner for giving expression to these forces. This settling is guided by the child's (now teenager's) "I," which is still working inwardly, preparing the way for taking true hold of the helm at age 21.

One addition, which is not actually part of this birthing process for the four members, but is very helpful to know about and recognize, is **the first moon node**. This comes approximately every 18 years and seven months (repeating at around ages 37, 56, and 74 years), when the sun and moon cross paths in the same place in the heavens as when one was first born. This repetition opens a window to a remembrance of the intention that first prompted one's incarnation. Questions such as, "How well does my life match what I am really supposed to be doing?" come forward. It brings the possibility for significant introspection and the potential for sober melancholy, but is often followed by the emergence of new courage and enthusiasm. In acts as a prelude to the greater step of "I" independence that comes with age 21, a kind of inner working of the "I."

Age 20–21 (the twenty-first year): the "I" becomes independent. A shift is now possible, not just away from the characteristics of the hereditary body (physical body), but also from the family and sometimes the culture (etheric body) of origin and from the social and emotional turmoil of adolescence (astral body). This step is in many ways the crowning achievement of childhood growth and development.

As liberated etheric forces make abstract, body-free thought possible, and liberated astral forces make more refined social and artistic sensitivity possible, so the liberation of "I" activity makes more independent and original intention possible. Questions related to the best ways to meet one's life task come to the fore ("What is my mission, my vocation?"). Moral sensing becomes more refined. Relationships shift as one is now better able to also sense the "I" of another human being. Experiences of the twenty-first year are different than the anxieties and insecurities of adolescence: The main task now relates to finding one's own truth rather than the more adolescent focus on finding one's place in relation to the outside world and social environment.

Development certainly continues beyond the twenty-first year. It carries a different flavor than the first three seven-year periods because adult development depends more on how we use and refine our capacities than on the process of birthing those capacities. The process of incarnation into the body reaches its fullest potential in the early thirties, with a turning point around the age of 33; from that point on we actually begin to lift, to excarnate some of our capacities out from their bodily tasks and into a more body-free state. What feel like later steps of physical decline are—viewed from another side—simply a birthing away from the body and back toward the spirit, just as the process of conception and birth into the physical world is a kind of death away from the spiritual world. By breathing more and more into this developmental weaving we can appreciate that we are all moving, all constantly changing. What we do not see—that which has not yet met the body, that which lives unconsciously at work in the body, or that which has been released from the body—still represents essential aspects of our humanity. We are simply able to see only on one side of the mirror. Observation of these rhythms offers small but vital glimpses of the full process.

ENDNOTES
1   Edmond Schoorel, "The Importance of the First Seven Years for the Rest of Life," in *The First Seven Years: Physiology of Childhood*. Fair Oaks, CA: Rudolf Steiner College Press, 2004.
2   Peter Selg, *Unbornness: Human Pre-existence and the Journey toward Birth*. Great Barrington, MA: SteinerBooks, 2010.
3   _____. *I Am Different from You: How Children Experience Themselves and the World in the Middle of Childhood*. Great Barrington, MA: SteinerBooks, 2011. Gives a really excellent physiologic and pedagogical picture of this important change.
4   Friedrich Husemann and Otto Wolff, *The Anthroposophical Approach to Medicine*, Volume 1. Spring Valley, NY: Anthroposophic Press. 1982.

Three Contributions to the Study of the Third Core Principle

CORE PRINCIPLE **3** *Developmental Curriculum*
The curriculum is created to meet and support the phase of development of the individual and the class. From birth to age 7 the guiding principle is that of imitation; from 7 to 14 the guiding principle is that of following the teacher's guidance; during the high school years the guiding principle is idealism and the development of independent judgment.

First Contribution
The Preschool and Kindergarten Years
Holly Koteen-Soulé

The curriculum of the Waldorf preschool and kindergarten is based on meeting the developmental needs of the child during the first seven-year cycle of life. During this phase, the healthy growth of the physical body and the development of the child's forces are primary and form a solid foundation for developments that will take place in the second and third seven-year cycles. While Waldorf early childhood programs can be found in over 60 countries and inevitably reflect the culture in which they exist, in this article we will explore common elements of the curriculum rather than specific variations.

Although Rudolf Steiner died before the founding of the first Waldorf kindergarten, he spoke about the unique qualities of the young child in many lecture cycles and offered several fundamental considerations for the education of the child from birth to seven years of age.

Learning by Imitation

A key statement in this Core Principle is that the young child learns by imitation. By this we understand that young children take in the world through sensory experiences, digest and integrate those experiences, and then reproduce what they have learned in some manner.[1] Imitation is also the means by which the child in the first three years (from the example of others) achieves the abilities to walk and speak and begins to think.[2]

Everything in the immediate environment leaves a deep impression on young children, especially the human beings who are close to them.[3] Based on this understanding, it is clear that the teachers themselves and their individual actions, words, and thoughts comprise a subtle, but important, aspect of the child's experience and the Waldorf early childhood curriculum. (See the Fifth Core Principle for more about how early childhood teachers work consciously to be worthy of imitation.) Waldorf early childhood educators meet the children in their care with warm-hearted empathy, are committed to self-development, and work out of a deep reverence for life.

Life, Work and Play

A more visible and recognizable element of the Waldorf early childhood curriculum is the focus on real, practical life, including daily, weekly, and seasonal activities. "The whole point of preschool is to give young children the opportunity to imitate life in a simple, wholesome way... [C]hildren transform adult occupations into child's play... [I]n children's imitation, in all their sense-directed activities, moral and spiritual forces are working—artistic impulses that allow the child to respond in an entirely individual manner."[4]

Ideally, the early childhood classroom is less like a school and more like a busy, bustling family home, in which the purposeful work of the adults and the play of the children weave together with warmth and joy. The teachers prepare meals, bake bread, make things for the classroom, wash, clean and mend, work in the garden, and connect with nature during outdoor excursions and in preparing for seasonal festivals. Depending on their age and abilities, children may help with the work, as well as bring it and other life experiences into their creative play. Work and play with natural materials and open-ended toys maximize the potential for sensory enrichment, experiential learning, and individual creativity. Seasonal activities are also experienced in an artistic way at circle time with movement games, songs, and verses.

The sense of home can be present regardless of whether the group gathers in a house, a school, or an outdoor shelter. Most Waldorf early childhood groups are comprised of children of mixed ages. This augments the sense of family, allows children to learn from one another, and helps them begin to develop a feeling for others and practice simple social skills. Social learning is not an overlay on the curriculum, but a natural, integral outcome of taking care of one's shared space and community.

Generally speaking, practical life activities can also support and stimulate the development of the basic senses of touch, life, movement, and balance, all of which are necessary for the healthy physical development during the first seven years.[5] In recent years, however, the lack of sufficient movement in our modern lifestyle requires that early childhood teachers work more consciously to make sure that children's needs for sensory development and integration are being met. Teachers may address these needs by bringing specific movements at circle time and by spending more time outside in nature.

The Benefits of Rhythm

So far we have explored two aspects that teachers consider in building their curriculum. First, everything in the environment, including the adults, should be worthy of imitation, and secondly, the activities of the classroom should be fully embedded in the practical life. Working out of both of these principles invites and welcomes the child to connect to his or her physical being and to the joy of life. A third important consideration has to do with providing support for the young child's learning to breathe.[6] In this case, "breathing" does not refer only to physical breathing. It also refers to bringing into balance or harmonizing opposing polarities, as in expanding and contracting or taking in and giving out. In this sense "breathing" is an important aspect of feeling at home in one's physical body and also relating to others and one's surroundings.

During the course of a day in a Waldorf early childhood classroom, there is a rhythmic alternation of child-initiated play and teacher-guided artistic activities, of expansive activity and focused activity, of vigorous movement and quiet rest, of speaking and listening, of verses and song, outdoor and indoor time, group activity and individual activity—all examples of moving between polarities. Taken from the perspective of the child, there is a sense of moving back and forth between a feeling of breathing out and a feeling of breathing in. The predictability of the daily rhythm provides security for the child. Over time, trust in the harmonizing flow between opposites creates a safe, bounded space where individuals and the group can feel free to engage in self-directed creative activity.

While life activities are the basis for the curriculum, self-initiated creative play is the heart of any Waldorf early childhood program. Successful creative play means that the children are transforming what they are experiencing of the world by their own will activity. In the process they are mastering their own will forces, so that those forces can support the development of their future feeling and thinking capacities.

Establishing Healthy Habits

The nature of the will forces in the young child and their development during the first seven years is a further aspect to consider in understanding the intentions of the Waldorf early childhood curriculum. Besides the already mentioned benefits of working rhythmically, a program based on regularly repeated activities organically guides the child's strong will impulses into healthy, useful habits.

The will of the child is the strongest during the first seven years. Between birth and approximately 2^1/3, the will is necessarily connected to the child's bodily instincts and impulses and is the quintessential *willing will*. Over the course of learning to walk and speak and beginning to think (between 2^1/3 and 4^2/3), the child is more open to others and the will has more of a desire character. This is sometimes called the *feeling will*. Between 4^2/3 and 7 years of age, when the child becomes more interested in the world, their will develops more of a motive character. This is sometimes called the *thinking will*.[7]

With the youngest children, working rhythmically supports the child's development of healthy physical habits in the areas of eating, dressing, and self-care. Between three and five years of age, clear, consistent rhythms and expectations can also support the development of healthy social habits, such as taking turns, sharing resources, and negotiating with others. With the older child in the kindergarten, habits arising from the opportunity to participate in purposeful work can be useful for one's life in many ways, including supporting future academic activities. All of these habits, of course, arise out of imitation and are strengthened by repetition and the teacher's rhythmic ordering of space and time.

These shifts in the quality of the will and the child's maturing physical capacities account for the different emphases that can be found in programs designed for children of a specific age range. Early childhood teachers often choose to bring in particular activities for the first-grade-ready children, as they near the end of their last year in kindergarten, in order to meet their burgeoning capacities and interests.

An Experiential Foundation for Numeracy and Literacy

A final common element of the Waldorf early childhood curriculum is the conscious awareness of helping the children build an experiential foundation for numeracy and literacy. Mathematical concepts are grasped organically in the course of everyday life activities, such as setting the table for snack and having to share or adding to limited resources for creative play. The telling of stories, fairy tales and puppetry build an artistic foundation for language development and literacy. This special aspect of the Waldorf early childhood curriculum also nourishes the still nascent soul life of the young child with dream-like pictures from the rich heritage of many world cultures.

ENDNOTES
1   Rudolf Steiner, *The Education of the Child in the Light of Spiritual Science*. Forest Row, UK: Rudolf Steiner Press, 1965, p.24.
2   _____, *The Child's Changing Consciousness and Waldorf Education*. Forest Row, UK: Rudolf Steiner Press, 1988, chs.2–3.
3   _____, *Human Values in Education*,. Great Barrington, MA: SteinerBooks, pp. 54–55.
4   Ibid., p.72.
5   Edmund Schoorel, *The First Seven Years: Physiology of Childhood*. Fair Oaks, CA: Rudolf Steiner College Press, ch.4.
6   Rudolf Steiner, *Study of Man*. Forest Row, UK: Rudolf Steiner Press, 1995, pp.20–22.
7   Renate Long-Breipohl, *Under the Stars: The Foundations of Steiner Waldorf Early Childhood Education*. Stroud, UK: Hawthorn Press, ch.3.

Second Contribution
The Grade School Years

James Pewtherer

As a child steps across the threshold from the nurturing routines of an early childhood space into the world of school, something new is now possible. It is at this time that the growth forces which had formed the young child are freed in some degree for use in a new way. At around age 7, those forces have completed a crucial phase of building the child's physical body and his or her organs. It is a foundational principle of child development and anthroposophically-informed education that these forces should not be called on prematurely for intellectual pursuits before this cycle of growth is complete. The aim is to ensure that a strong, healthy physical body will be there as a foundation for the child's entire life before these growth forces begin to be redirected in service of focused, cognitive activity.

Working with these freed-up forces, the class teacher now gradually weans the child from much of the imitative learning that characterizes early childhood education. In its place, the child delves into the world of images, where the imagination leads over into understanding. The children hear a beautifully-told story or see a chalk drawing on the board, and while absorbed as they take in these things, they begin to be more reflective about these inner and outer pictures, comparing their experiences in discussions about what they have heard or seen. They should still love what they see, but now they do so with more distance than did the kindergarten child. At this age, the child can begin to put those pictures into a context or what we can call a growing "understanding." This understanding, however, is more than abstract, intellectual knowledge. Instead, it is understanding saturated with rich feelings that run the gamut from excitement to sadness to joy. In this way, the learning during the years of the elementary school should never become dried out and dead. The gradual separation of "self" from "world" in these early elementary school years must not make the child feel isolated from the world. Instead, at the end of a lesson, the child should be left with the enthusiastic feeling, "That was so interesting and exciting! I want to learn more!"

An overarching principle that is developmentally appropriate in a child's education during this second seven-year period includes the love of one's teacher, the love of learning, and the recognition of the beauty to be found in the world. It is up to the teacher to provide the example as artist, scientist, and beloved guide. These qualities in the teacher cultivate in the child a feeling life that in turn develops a trust in his or her own heart-borne judgment. This is one of the imponderables that grows imperceptibly during these elementary years. It leads the child to know that his/her own heart is increasingly able to be a true guide as to the right way to act in a given situation. This is a matter of cultivating authentic sensibilities, feelings that will help children develop a moral compass rather than maudlin sentimentality. It is the teacher who guides this development through his or her relationship to and love for the individual child and the class as a whole, ideally over a span of eight school years.

During the initial phase of this seven-year period, for instance in the first grade, the teacher may tell a story of four animals who decide to unite in seeking a new life for themselves in the town of Bremen. The child can see that each animal has its one-sidedness, in that the donkey is good at one thing and the cat at something else. But when the animals join forces, the child sees how their collaboration leads them to succeed where, on their own, they would have failed.

Once the story has been told, and the children have been able to sleep on it, they re-create it by retelling it out of their own internal, imaginative pictures. Then, in a completely non-didactic way, a conversation ensues based on their simple observations about how one of the characters acted or the way events unfolded. Inherent in such a story is also a living picture of how the human being combines many of these traits to become truly human. Yet such a concept is not spoken. Rather it would stand there, ready for the children to draw upon it then or at some later time in the years to come. They gain a feeling for the "rightness" of such a reality.

The middle years of the elementary school time provide still more illustrations of this developmental approach. One of these arises in arithmetic when working with common fractions. By their very nature, numbers are abstractions in that they take the child from a consideration of objects (e.g., apples) to "counters" that stand for the objects (e.g., fingers, strokes on a page, etc.) and finally to symbols (4 or 57 or 2398). Imagine, then: How does a ten-year-old in fourth grade make sense of a fractional (broken) number which has a 3 over a 4 (3/4) or a 5 over a 16 (5/16)? And then how does the child make sense of the concept that the "4" in the first example is a bigger number than the "16" in the second one?

Here the sure-handed teacher leads the children through all sorts of cutting-out exercises and practices, using regular paper shapes or blocks of wood or slices of pizza. We take them apart and put them together; we try to combine equal and then different "sizes" (denominators) and different quantities ("numerators") of the fractions (3 fourths and 1 fourth; then 3 eighths and 5 eighths; then 1 fourth and 1 eighth, etc.). Stories are invented to illustrate the use of these pieces in addition to games that require putting together or taking apart these pieces to make mixed numbers and/or find common denominators. Only then can the abstraction of number have a sufficient foundation in experience to allow the child to feel comfort and success in working with these abstractions and in further computations with them.

Here it is important to note the shift in consciousness which most children experience at the age of about 9. For at the time of this oft-called "nine-year change" in third or fourth grade, the child necessarily finds that the unity of the world, which was a given up until then, is gradually lost. (This is one of the reasons that introducing fractions—"broken numbers"—is so apt at this age.) While this loss of childhood wholeness is a kind of crisis for a child, it is an important step toward freedom in his/her development. The children become aware of differences among themselves, of the fallibility of parents and teachers, and of the hard work needed to achieve the results they want in their own work. At the same time, a feeling of vulnerability and insecurity comes over the child, leading to critical comments about adults and other children, attempts to prove his/her competence or superiority, and a wish to be reassured that he/she is loved and valued.

So it is critical that the sure hand of the wise teacher guides the children through this crisis. It is the inspired teacher who must decide what to bring to the class at every given moment and how best to bring it. The genius of the education can meet the needs of the children in a number of ways. At this age, these include: curricula which give an imaginative picture of the pathway to becoming true human beings (e.g., in Old Testament stories) and practical studies which teach them that human efforts, that is, their efforts, can provide food, clothing and shelter for people. They can predictably and consistently know some aspects of the world around them through using weight and measure to gauge their surroundings. They can learn the satisfaction of repeatedly overcoming their own imperfections through hard work and patience in order to create things of beauty. Not of least importance is also the loving but firm expectations of the teacher who requires of each child that he/she live up to the truly human standards of care, politeness, kindness, and fair play in how the child meets others and meets the world.

Towards the end of the elementary years, in another example, the subject of modern history provides the teacher with yet another opportunity to give the children a chance to experience themselves as stepping into the stream of human society. Biographies of larger-than-life personalities such as Gandhi, Mother Theresa, and Martin Luther King, Jr., can be joined by those of little-known heroes such as "Wild Bill Cody" (who survived the Nazi concentration camps) or the Japanese engineer who in 2013 led his workers out of the black horror and sure death of the tsunami-stricken Fukushima nuclear power plant. Inventors, natural scientists, astronomers—individuals in virtually every walk of life—can provide examples of what it means to learn about oneself and the world so as to rise to one's true humanity.

In these upper-elementary history classes, the students widen their focus from their own (often egotistical) concerns at this age to also see their place in the world. The teacher uses the subject matter to awaken them to humanity's charge to become part of the solution to what ails us in society today. They have experienced the range of gifts and challenges embodied in their long-time classmates as well as in their own communities at home. Out of this, they are coming to feel their individual responsibility to take initiative and help others in their community. They also come to see their enhanced effectiveness when working together with others and in a healthy group of peers.

These elementary years embrace another stage of development, the so-called "twelve-year change," which takes place toward later elementary school years. At this time, the physical body begins to change outwardly with its longer limbs and development of secondary sexual characteristics. The bony structure becomes more prominent, the voices of the boys drop, breasts in the girls develop, and the sense of having a private, inner life grows stronger in both genders. Here it is important to pull their singular focus away from their own naturally egotistical concerns and have them learn about the myriad matters of interest and need in the world around them.

The aim is to teach them so that these older children are moved to want to do something out of their own initiative, even if they haven't yet developed the analytical ability to stand back, see, and then understand what is called for out of a wider context. That ability and awareness will develop in the high school years. Here, the task of the class and subject teachers is to keep them inspired and working to develop their own knowledge of self and world. The point is that they come to feel more inspired to want to learn and to work for positive change in themselves and the world. The curriculum as well as the love and respect of the children for their teachers provide the means to educate the growing human being at this stage of development.

By the end of the elementary school years, the class teacher has helped them to develop a healthy relationship to self-knowledge and knowledge of the world around them. Now, as the class teacher steps back, a circle of high school teachers takes up the care of the young person as the individual personality emerges further. The knowledge which was brought through image and feeling life is now enhanced by a schooling of the emergent ability to think in the next stage of development in the high school years.

Third Contribution
The High School Years
Douglas Gerwin

> Some say the world will end in fire,
> Some say in ice.[1]
> > – Robert Frost

In a lecture entitled "Education for Adolescents," Rudolf Steiner describes how, from puberty onwards, "latent questions" begin rising in the minds of young adults concerning all aspects of life in the world. Steiner says that the teacher must help adolescents articulate these questions—without, however, falling into the trap of answering them—"so that riddles arise in their youthful souls."[2]

If riddles do not come to consciousness in the growing teenager, then the soul forces that would normally give rise to these life questions run the risk of being diverted in two directions: toward a lust for the erotic or toward a lust for power. In other words, with puberty a creative urge awakens in teenagers that can realize itself in both senses of the verb "to conceive"—that is, in the capacity to give birth to abstract ideas as well as the capacity to create new human life. Starting with this age, we are able to conceive our own thoughts no less than our own offspring. If these burgeoning powers of abstract thinking—a thinking saturated, to be sure, with deep feeling and yearning for ideals—are thwarted, then they may be redirected to one or the other form of lust.

Though they share a common origin, the lust for the erotic and the lust for power manifest themselves in the human soul as opposites. The lust for the erotic may be felt as erupting out of deep and mysterious depths, like a volcano overwhelming the conscious mind with feelings that carry the searing heat of desire:

> From what I've tasted of desire
> I hold with those who favor fire.[3]

By contrast, the lust for power may be felt as a powerful intellectual force of cognition descending as though from above, taking hold of our will with an icy, calculating intention born of cold hatred.

> But if it had to perish twice,
> I think I know enough of hate
> To say that for destruction ice
> Is also great
> And would suffice.[4]

Generalizations are risky, but boys are probably more likely to divert this creative intellectual energy into a pursuit of the physical eroticism, girls into the pursuit of psychological power. You will more often discover pornographic magazines hidden beneath the beds of the boys, for example, than of the girls, and the legion of X-rated sites on the internet is far more geared to lure male than female visitors. On the other side of the sexual divide, the sometimes catty and even cruel behavior more typical of young adolescent girls may be understood as an expression of a lust for power.

It is important, though, to remember that both erotic and power lusts originate in the same capacity of soul—namely, in the capacity to conceive. In this context, one may ask how this capacity can be exercised without being prematurely drawn into physical expression or behavioral perversion.

Here Rudolf Steiner points to the redemptive value of beauty for engaging the erotic sense before it is diverted into the sensual and to the value of deeds of altruism in harnessing the lust for power before it is turned to selfish purpose. Ultimately, lusts of any kind stimulate a craving that can never be satisfied. In contrast, experiences of beauty and altruism yield nourishment that is deeply and lastingly satisfying.

For insight into the more general latent questions that live just below adolescent consciousness, we may turn to the Waldorf high school curriculum and the riddles it can inspire. In their specifics, these questions will take on an individual character in the mind and heart of each teenager who poses them. But in general it is perhaps possible to identify four simple yet archetypal questions that are bound to arise, and which the Waldorf high school curriculum is designed to address at each level of a student's four-year high school career.

Each year of the Waldorf high school curriculum embodies, in broad strokes, an underlying question or theme that helps guide students, not just through their studies of outer phenomena, but through their inner growth as well. These themes and methods are adapted to each specific group of students and take account of the fact that teenagers mature at varying paces—hence the "broad strokes." And yet, one can identify struggles common to most any teenager. Even though adolescents pass through developmental landscapes at varying speeds, they all nonetheless will cover similar terrain.

Grade Nine

As freshmen plunge into the high school, they are also plunging with new intensity into the materiality of their bodies—with the unfolding of puberty—and into the immateriality of abstract thinking. There is tension in this opposition, often struggle, and occasionally even revolt.

The ninth grade curriculum is designed with these tremendous developmental changes and struggles in mind. It allows the students to see their inner experiences reflected to them in outer phenomena. In physics, for instance, students study in thermodynamics the opposition of heat and cold; in chemistry, the expansion and contraction of gases; in history, the conflicts and the resulting revolutions in the United States, France, Russia, China, and Iran; and in geology, the collision of plate tectonics.

Through the chaos and tension of these struggles, students are summoned to exercise powers of exact observation: in the sciences, to describe and draw precisely what happened in the lab experiments and demonstrations (without adding, from the outset, an overlay of theoretical explanation); in the humanities, to recount clearly a sequence of events or to describe the nature of a character without getting lost in a plethora of details. The objective here is to train in the students powers of exact observation and reflection so that they can experience in the raging storm of phenomena around them the steady ballast of their own thinking. Strong powers of wakeful perception form the basis for later years of study, well beyond high school.

One may summarize the content and approach of this freshman curriculum with the underlying question: **What?** *What happened? What's going on here? What did you see and hear?*

Grade Ten

Emerging from the turmoil of grade nine, the tenth grader may begin to discover a certain balance point between the violent collision of opposites. Physically, the boys may achieve a steadier gait as their legs thicken and catch up with their oversized feet, while the girls may appear more poised and upright. Mentally, the sophomores may begin to bring a certain order to the confusion of their thoughts, a calming mid-point to the turbulence of opposites.

The curriculum responds to this search with subjects that incorporate the comparison and balancing of contrasting opposites: in chemistry, the study of acids and bases; in physics, the principles of mechanics; in earth sciences, the self-regulating processes of weather patterns; in astronomy, the co-equality of centripetal and centrifugal forces; in embryology, the play of masculine and feminine influences.

Through the study of balance in natural and human phenomena, students can begin to find their own fulcrum. In so doing, they are called to exercise powers of comparison and contrast, weighing in the balance contrary phenomena to determine their value and significance, as well as their origin.

Students may discover that in this balancing of opposites, new forms can arise—in clouds and tides, or in planets and solar systems, or in male and female sexuality. This discovery may in turn prompt the desire to explore the origins of things, to find the source of these forms in the beginnings of the universe or of history or of human language. In other words, the study of ancient times can now be taken up at a deeper level.

One may summarize the themes of this grade with the underlying question: **How?** *How does this relate to that? How do these contrasting phenomena interrelate? And how did they come about?*

Grade Eleven

As adolescents enter the second half of their high school career, generalizations about their development become increasingly difficult. The strokes must grow ever broader. "Sweet sixteen" and beyond, however, is a typical time of newfound depths to the inner life of thoughts, feelings, and deeds. Deeper— and more individualized—latent questions may begin to burn. This may be the year in which students feel the urge to change schools or even to drop out of school altogether. In these inner promptings, a new and urgent voice speaks: "Leave behind what you have been given and get on with your own journey!" Inner yearnings for intellectual independence and freedom from parental or environmental constraints may drive teenagers of this age into avenues of private pursuit and personal interests very different from what up until now has occupied them. Outer statements of growing independence (already visible in earlier years) may also abound—in dress, hairstyles, the pursuit of part-time jobs, and what used to be the most exciting and sometimes premature token of maturity—the driver's license.[5]

The curriculum for the junior year allows students to cut free to a greater degree from their peers and set off on their own uncharted course into the invisible recesses of life within. The junior year curriculum could be characterized by the theme of "invisibility": namely, by the study of those subjects that draw the student into areas not accessible to the experience of our senses.

Such a journey requires a new type of thinking—thinking no longer anchored in what our senses give us—as well as a feeling of confidence that this type of thinking will not lead us astray.

In literature, for instance, this journey to an invisible source is captured in main lesson blocks such as the Grail legends or Dante's *Divine Comedy*. Other subjects, however, call upon similar powers. In chemistry, the students enter the invisible kingdom of the atom (invisible because, by definition, one cannot "see" atoms). In physics, they explore the invisible world of electricity (which we can perceive only in its effects, not in its inherent nature). In history, they relive Medieval, Renaissance, and Enlightenment eras in which men and women set off on individual quests and journeys to destinations unknown (and, in some cases, unknowable). In projective geometry, we follow parallel lines to the point they share in the infinite—a point that can be thought even though it cannot be pictured.

In short, like the horizon that beckoned to Renaissance explorers like Magellan, calling them to venture beyond its visible edge, the dimensions of the classroom during the junior year are vastly enlarged to embrace the furthest reaches of the student's own imagination and interests. In many aspects of the curriculum, the student is launched into more ambitious, individual projects, and research assignments.

These voyages to the invisible landscapes pose an underlying question intended to strengthen the student's powers of independent analysis and abstract theorizing. The question is: **Why?** *Why are things this way? Why did the events of history take this or that course?* And even deeper "why" questions— *Why am I here?*, questions of destiny, life's meaning, social responsibility—may find their way into the classroom at this age.

Grade Twelve

The twelve years of Waldorf education can be compared to a giant cylindrical tower set in a vast expanse of landscape. One can imagine children entering at the ground level of this tower in first grade and beginning to climb an interior spiral staircase of eleven turns. At each level (or floor) of the tower, they can look out through a window that gives a partial perspective of the surrounding landscape. Some curricular "windows" are set above one another, at different levels of the spiral staircase. For example, the "windows" for grade eight and grade nine look out at the same landscape but from different heights.

Approaching the twelfth grade level, the seniors push open a trap door in the roof of the tower and step out onto an open terrace. Now, for the first time, they can survey the full panorama of the landscape that they previously glimpsed on the way up through eleven preceding perspectives. In other words, the senior year is intended to be the gradual synthesis of the education— the great stock-taking and preparation for the next stage in learning—and also, the fully conscious placement of oneself in the center of this panorama.

"Point" and "periphery" are the complementary perspectives for this year. The senior curriculum serves both by offering subjects that synthesize many themes—world history, architecture, *Faust*—and relate these themes to the centrality of the human being, as well as to current times. To the same end, the students study the relationship of the human being to the varied animal kingdoms (zoology). They read the Transcendentalists, Russian novelists, such as Dostoyevski, and other great thinkers and writers who have wrestled with modern questions of our place in today's world.

Assignments increasingly call upon the students to integrate what they have studied, to synthesize disparate disciplines in an attempt to address the underlying question of the senior curriculum: **Who?** *Who is this being that is called Human? And ultimately—Who stands behind the outer play of events and natural phenomena, integrating them in a synthesizing whole?*

In this sense, the curriculum of the twelfth grade not only recapitulates the themes of the four years of high school, but also returns to the place where the Waldorf curriculum began in grade one—with the image of the whole. Now, however, the difference, one hopes, is that the student will truly "know the place for the first time."

In summary:

Grade nine, by training powers of *observation*, speaks to the underlying question: **What?**

Grade ten, by training powers of *comparison*, speaks to the underlying question: **How?**

Grade eleven, by training powers of *analysis*, speaks to the underlying question: **Why?**

Grade twelve, by training powers of *synthesis*, speaks to the underlying question: **Who?**

By means of these broad and archetypal questions, high school students are invited to explore the fathomless riddles of their surroundings and of their own existence, starting in the breadth of the outer world—the world of "What Is"—and culminating in the depths of the inner world—the world of "Who Is." Ultimately it is these questions that will guide them in the pursuit of their creative conceptions, both intellectual and sexual.

ENDNOTES

1 Robert Frost, "Fire and Ice" in *Complete Poems of Robert Frost*. New York: Holt, Rinehart and Winston, 1964, p.268.

2 Rudolf Steiner, "Education for Adolescents" (21 June 1922), reprinted in *Genesis of a Waldorf High School: A Source Book*, ed. Douglas Gerwin, 3rd edition. Fair Oaks, CA: AWSNA Publications, 2001, pp.3–6. This lecture should not be confused with the lecture cycle which Rudolf Steiner gave to the Waldorf teachers a year earlier and which was initially known as "The Supplementary Course" (because it followed up on the lecture course entitled *Study of Man*) and which has since been published under various titles including *Education for Adolescents*. Hudson, NY: Anthroposophic Press, 1996.

3 Op. cit., Robert Frost, p.268

4 Ibid.

5 Whereas the receipt of the first driver's license used to be perhaps the most important rite of passage for the adolescent, nowadays in the age of internet and virtual friendships, somewhere between a quarter and a third of eligible teenagers are forgoing the option of getting their driver's permit. Instead, they rely on their parents— or on rides arranged via social media—to get around.

A Contribution to the Study of the Fourth Core Principle

Jennifer Snyder

CORE PRINCIPLE 4 *Freedom in Teaching*
Rudolf Steiner gave indications for the development of a new pedagogical art, with the expectation that "the teacher must invent this art at every moment." Out of the understanding of child development and Waldorf pedagogy, the Waldorf teacher is expected to meet the needs of the children in the class out of his/her insights and the circumstances of the school. Interferences with the freedom of the teacher by the school, parents, standardized testing regimens, or the government, while they may be necessary in a specific circumstance (for safety or legal reasons, for example), are nonetheless compromises.[1]

> How can we ourselves transform education for the free human being into a free act in the very highest sense, that is to say, into a moral act? How can education become out and out a moral concern of mankind? This is the great problem before us today, and it must be solved if the most praiseworthy efforts toward educational reform are to be rightly directed on into the future. (Rudolf Steiner, *Education*, Lecture 3)

Rudolf Steiner spoke these words over 90 years ago to inspire a new art of pedagogy, and they are possibly more urgent for us to grapple with today. In the United States, it has instead become the norm for educational reform to issue from the dictates of legislative authority rather than from experienced educators. Restrictions on the freedom of individual educators have become the populist standard.

In all areas of cultural life, institutions are facing restrictions on their freedom imposed or threatened to be imposed by political legislation. This is as true for the practice of medicine, for example, as it is for education. The autonomous "country doctor," who was once able to practice medicine guided solely by the Hippocratic Oath, now has to operate within the confines of predetermined protocols. The ethics and competence of individual doctors were traditionally determined only by the opinions of their peers. Hospitals granted doctors wide-ranging autonomy to practice the highest form of medicine. Today physicians have exchanged much of that autonomy for protection against a litigious society.

Parallel to the compromises in the autonomy of the practicing physician is a challenge to the freedom of the modern educator. The Core Principle defending "Freedom in Teaching" stands as a lighthouse to guide the journey of the contemporary teacher on the stormy seas of current educational practices.

The path of the developing Waldorf teacher could be compared to that of a jazz musician who is becoming an artisan working within a live form. Subtle improvised changes to a "standard" or set form, made in the moment and responsive to the others in the ensemble, characterize "jazz" music. True jazz music is rarely played as written and does not exist until played in live performance. Yet, to get to this ethereal place, improvisation cannot be interjected for its own sake, or else the song risks losing integrity. True masters can play the same song, and it will always be different, yet we will all still recognize the tune. Similarly, no two master jazz musicians will ever be expected to play a piece of music the same way. The novice Waldorf teacher working with the core principle of "Freedom in Teaching" should recognize that it is not a license for performing "free form expressionism" with the lesson. Analogous to the journey of novice musicians developing their craft, the teacher must learn from performing standards.

A jazz performer can apprentice, or play with a master of the form, to develop greater chops. So too can the developing Waldorf teacher. Performing could be considered a meaningful career path for a musician both in live gigs and in the recording studio. On the other hand, the unique and rare gift of incredible jazz playing arises out of a synergy among an ensemble of musicians who share a deep background in the form and structure of music, along with finely-tuned craftsmanship and the ineffable quality of "free" spirit.

Rudolf Steiner offered the original circle of Waldorf teachers many thoughts to inspire this new pedagogical art, always hoping that in the mastery of this new form, freedom would arise out of deepest morality as the genesis of the art.

Taken in the order in which they appear, there are six primary thoughts expressed in this Core Principle. To begin, here are relevant quotes from the work of Rudolf Steiner to substantiate each thought:

1) Rudolf Steiner gave indications for developing a new pedagogical art.

> And in the practice of teaching, there will awaken in us, out of this knowledge of human nature, the art of education in a quite individual form. (*Balance in Teaching*, Lecture 3)

> We have to lead an education into the future. This makes it necessary that in our present epoch the whole

situation of education must be different from what it was in the past. (*Education*, Lecture 3)

In principle it is possible to introduce Waldorf education anywhere, because it is based purely on pedagogy. This is the significant difference between Waldorf pedagogy and other educational movements.

Waldorf education focuses entirely on the pedagogical aspect; it can be adapted to any outer conditions, whether a city school, a country school or whatever. It is not designed to meet specific external conditions, but is based entirely on observation and insight into the growing human being. This means that Waldorf pedagogy could be implemented in every school. (*The Child's Changing Consciousness*, Lecture 8)

We concern ourselves not only with teaching methods, but particularly with creating the curriculum and teaching goals from a living observation of growing children. This art of education requires that we fit it exactly to what develops in a human being. We should derive what we call the curriculum and educational goals from that. What we teach and how we teach should flow from an understanding of human beings. (*Spiritual Science and Pedagogy: A Lecture for Public School Teachers*, 1919)

It is meaningful to refer to the concept of a "standard curriculum" in Waldorf education, and to acknowledge that the novice teacher is not expected to improvise like a jazz master. The songs can be played as written, at least to the degree that they are committed to writing.

2) The teacher, rather than a theory or institution, is accepted as the central author of this new art of education.

That is why the Waldorf school came into being in such a way that there were no set principles or systems—only children and teachers. We have to consider not only the individuality of every single child, but the individuality of every single teacher as well. We must know our teachers. It is easy to draft rules and principles that tell teachers what to do and not do. But what matters is the capacities of individual teachers and the development of their capacities; they do not need educational precepts, but a knowledge of the human being that takes them into life itself and considers whole persons in a living way. (*The Roots of Education*, Lecture 4)

Everything depends upon the personality of the teacher. This comes out quite clearly throughout the whole lecture, with warmth, depth and responsibility. Time and again it made me particularly happy that Dr. Steiner emphasized this with complete insight and certainty. Thus, he has also shown us what a great task and responsibility we have if we wish to continue in our profession as teachers. (*Spiritual Science and Pedagogy: A Lecture for Public School Teachers*, 1919, from a teacher in the audience after the lecture)

Returning to the analogy of the jazz musician to the teacher, the art arises from the artist because it is always performed live. Children reside in the present moment, and that is where art can arise.

3) The ingenuity of the teacher in every moment is the ideal of a living, evolving pedagogy.

In educating, what the teacher does can depend only slightly on anything he gets from a general, abstract pedagogy; it must rather be newly born every moment from a living understanding of the young human being he or she is teaching. (*An Introduction to Waldorf Education, An Essay*)

In order for pedagogy to be general for humanity, teachers must practice it as an individual and personal art. ...

The developing human thus becomes a divine riddle for us, a divine riddle that we wish to solve at every hour. If, with our art of teaching, we so place ourselves in the service of humanity, then we serve this life from our great interest in life. (*Spiritual Science and Pedagogy: A Lecture for Public School Teachers*, 1919)

Once again, the kernel of the matter is knowing how to adapt to the individuality of the growing child. (*The Child's Changing Consciousness*, Lecture 6)

4) When the teacher perceives the processes of child development in the student(s), individual moments of changing consciousness can be understood, and the requisite pedagogy can arise.

On the one hand, we stand on the firm ground of pedagogy that derives from objective knowledge, and that prescribes specific curricular and educational tasks for each year. To ascertain what must be done in this education, we take our cue from the children themselves; and not only for each year, but also for each month, each week, and in the end, each day. ... [Teachers] have come to realize that not a single detail of this pedagogy is arbitrary, that everything in it is a response to what can be read in the child's own nature. (*The Child's Changing Consciousness*, Lecture 7)

It is true that to bring the two into harmony—the development of the pupil and the development of the civilized world—will require a body of teachers who do not shut themselves up in an educational routine with strictly professional interests, but rather take an active interest in the whole range of life. Such a body of teachers will discover how to awaken in the upcoming generation a sense of the inner, spiritual substance of life and also an understanding of life's practicalities. (*An Introduction to* Waldorf Education, *An Essay*)

The first thing that was imparted to the teachers of the Waldorf School in the seminary course was a fundamental knowledge of man. Thus it was hoped that from an understanding of the true nature of man they would gain inner enthusiasm and love for education. For when one understands the human being, the very best thing for the practice of education must spring forth from this knowledge. Pedagogy is love for man resulting from knowledge of man; at all events it is only on this foundation that it can be built up. (*Education*, Lecture 5)

5) Teachers are called upon to develop unique insights out of their inner work and perceptions.

It is now planned that the Waldorf School will be a primary school in which the educational goals and

73

curriculum are founded upon each teacher's living insight into the nature of the whole human being, so far as this is possible under present conditions. (*An Introduction to Waldorf Education, An Essay*)

The world is permeated by spirit, and true knowledge of the world must be permeated by spirit as well. Anthroposophy can give us spiritual knowledge of the world, and, with it, spiritual knowledge of the human being, and this alone leads to a true education. (*The Roots of Education*, Lecture 2)

The child accepts the teacher's opinion and feeling because they live in the teacher. There must be something in the way the teacher meets the child that acts as an intangible. There must be something that really flows from an all-encompassing understanding of life and from the interest in an all-encompassing understanding of life. I have characterized it by saying that what we impart to children often reveals itself in a metamorphosed form only in the adult, or even in old age. (*Spiritual Science and Pedagogy: A Lecture for Public School Teachers*, 1919)

6) Compromises result from "prevailing conditions" of one's school or situation.

It would be fatal if the educational views upon which the Waldorf School is founded were dominated by a spirit out of touch with life. (*An Introduction to Waldorf Education, An Essay*)

Sectarianism to any degree or fanatical zeal must never be allowed to creep into our educational endeavors, only to find at the end of the road that our students do not fit into life as it is; for life in the world does not notice one's educational ideals. Life is governed by what arises from the prevailing conditions themselves, which are expressed as regulations concerning education, as school curricula, and as other related matters, which correspond to current ways of thinking. And so there is always a danger that we will educate children in a way that, though correct in itself, could alienate them from life in the world— whether one considers this right or wrong. It must always be remembered that one must not steer fanatically toward one's chosen educational aims without considering whether or not one might be alienating one's students from surrounding life. ...

From the very beginning of the Waldorf school something had to be done. It is difficult to give it a proper name, but something bad or negative had to be agreed upon—that is, a kind of compromise—simply because this school is not grounded in fanaticism but in objective reality. At the very beginning, a memorandum addressed to the local school authorities had to be worked out. ... Such an offer, for our teachers, amounted to an "ingratiating compromise"—forgive the term, I cannot express it otherwise. A realistic mind has to take such a course, for discretion is essential in everything one does. A fanatic would have responded differently. (*The Child's Changing Consciousness,* Lecture 7)

Idealism must work in the spirit of [the school's] curriculum and methodology; but it must be an idealism that has the power to awaken in young, growing human beings the forces and faculties they will need in later life to be equipped for work in modern society and to obtain for themselves an adequate living. The pedagogy and instructional methodology will be able to fulfill this requirement only through a genuine knowledge of the developing human being. (*An Introduction to Waldorf Education, An Essay*)

Now that we have identified these key thoughts in Steiner's work, let us look at educational freedom from another perspective.

Academic freedom is not unique to Waldorf education. As Ralph Fuchs (1963) notes, it is given out to members of the academic community and underlies "the effective performance of their functions of teaching, learning, practice of the arts, and research." It is considered a right, and "it is not sought as a personal privilege, although scholars enjoy the activities it permits," which "resemble that of the judge who holds office during good behavior to safeguard his fearlessness and objectivity in the performance of his duties."

This concept of freedom within academia in the United States rests upon a three-part foundation:

» Originating in Greek philosophy, it arises again in Europe during the Renaissance, and still later comes to maturity during the Age of Reason;
» It arises as a function of autonomy for communities of scholars in the earliest universities of Europe;
» It appears as a guarantee in the Bill of Rights of the Federal Constitution as elaborated by the courts.[2]

Freedom in teaching granted within Waldorf education can thus be placed in a context of classical Western academic philosophy, in which responsibility and autonomy are granted to the educator. We can begin to understand that the significance of Rudolf Steiner's idea of freedom within education, as illustrated in this core principle, reflects the classical role of the educator.

Today, however, latitude for the individual teacher in mainstream education—both secular and parochial—is reserved only for higher levels of education; in contrast, in Waldorf education freedom is extended to educators at all levels of instruction.

> For Rudolf Steiner (1861–1925), a full comprehension
> of freedom and its correct application in life lay at
> the heart of human morality and development, and
> as a solution to the most pertinent problems afflicting
> mankind. He did not mean the freedom to follow
> one's animal drives and passions, but rather freeing
> the human being from such tyrannies, of allowing
> the self to rise to greater heights of perception and
> insight into supersensible realms and the leading
> of moral life. Upon the possibility of liberating the
> individual's consciousness from material to spiritual
> reality through self-perception, Steiner founded the
> principles of Anthroposophy: the spiritual science of
> the human soul.[3]

In coming to understand the meaning that Rudolf Steiner imparts to the controversial term "freedom," one arrives on the shore of ancient pedagogical practice. The call for teachers to realize freedom in education is an imperative if modern pedagogical art is to continue to be grounded in the principles of classical education.

> If one studies education as a science consisting of all
> sorts of principles and formulas, it means about the
> same thing in terms of education as choosing to eat
> partially digested foods. But if we undertake a study of
> the child, of the true nature of the human being, and
> learn to understand children in this way, we take into
> ourselves the equivalent of what nature offers us as

nourishment. And in the practice of teaching there will awaken in us, out of this knowledge of human nature, the art of education in a quite individual form. In reality the teacher must invent this art every moment. (*Balance in Teaching*, Lecture 3)

When the issue of freedom is discussed in Waldorf schools, frequently questions arise concerning consistency and quality control. "What do I tell parents who ask me why their children's class teachers are teaching different lessons at the same age?" asks the enrollment director, or, "If every teacher can choose what to do, then how do you know that they are teaching well and how can you get them to change if they have to change?"

These concerns require answers, but the answers should arise out of discussion and collaboration, like a jazz musician working out of an ensemble, rather than out of some external entity enforcing regulations on the practicing teachers. "External" in this sense can even be the school's own guidelines. Without a doubt, the school has to be able to stand behind what the teachers are doing. Yet the more this "standing behind" is based on written protocols and predetermined solutions, the more compromised can be the pedagogy. Experienced teachers should engage newer ones (and one another) in conversations about the aims and methods of the school, and should visit each other's classrooms to ascertain that Waldorf pedagogy is being practiced successfully. A teacher may have to make changes, and indeed few are the teachers who do not need to shift perspectives or make changes. And if a teacher refuses to cooperate with the school leadership, then that lack of cooperation becomes a separate issue and may lead to corrective action. An important point to remember is that freedom and license are not the same, and that the results of a teacher's work must stand up to the scrutiny of his or her peers. Ultimately, however, the ideal is a faculty composed of responsible and capable teachers who are able to find what their students need without having to follow a predetermined path.

Perhaps the strongest argument in favor of the principle of freedom in teaching is that Waldorf education bills itself as an education toward freedom, and it is absurd to suggest that we can educate "free human beings, who are able of themselves to impart direction and meaning to their lives" while at the same time following a scripted approach to education. As difficult as it is to stand under the authority of one's own pedagogical judgment, it is what we must finally strive to accomplish in creating this art.

ENDNOTES

1   A note about school governance: While not directly a pedagogical matter, school governance can be an essential aspect of freedom in teaching. Just as a developmental curriculum should support the phases of child development, school governance should support the teachers' pedagogical freedom (while maintaining the school's responsibilities toward society).

2   See Ralph Fuchs' "Academic Freedom: Its Basic Philosophy, Function, and History," 28 *Law and Contemporary Problems*, pp.431-446 (Summer 1963). Available at: http://scholarship.law.duke.edu/lcp/vol28/iss3/2

3   Chris Fort, "How Esoteric Is Rudolf Steiner's Concept of Freedom?" with special reference to his *Philosophy of Freedom*, 2010. Available at http://www.academia.edu/537155/How_Esoteric_is_Rudolf_Steiners_Concept_of_Freedom_With_Special_Reference_to_his_Philosophy_of_Freedom

A Contribution to the Study of the Fifth Core Principle

James Pewtherer

CORE PRINCIPLE **5** *Methodology of Teaching*

There are a few key methodological guidelines for the grade school and high school teachers. Early childhood teachers work with these principles appropriate to the way in which the child before the age of 7 learns—that is, out of imitation rather than direct instruction:

> » Artistic metamorphosis: The teacher should understand, internalize, and then present the topic in an artistic form.[1]
> » From experience to concept: The direction of the learning process should proceed from the students' soul activities of willing through feeling to thinking. In the high school, the context of the experience is provided at the outset.[2]
> » Holistic process: proceeding from the whole to the parts and back again, and addressing the whole human being.
> » Use of rhythm and repetition.[3]

Holly Koteen-Soulé writes about early childhood: Before the age of 7, children are deeply impressed by everything in their surroundings, especially by the human beings with whom they have a close connection. They learn by taking in, integrating and reproducing their experiences through the inherent capacity of imitation. (See the Third Core Principle for a fuller description of the principle of imitation.)

All of the guidelines indicated above in the Fifth Core Principle (that are so helpful in understanding how the Waldorf educator works with the grades or high school student) have been embedded into the classroom environment and the rhythmic flow of the day, week, and year or internalized by the early childhood teachers. What the child experiences in the early childhood setting should be a sense of the wholeness of life, rather than its separate parts. The teacher guides the children's experiences out of his or her own artistic transformation of life's essential lessons.

Because this is the case, it is not so easy to tease apart the ways in which the Waldorf early childhood educator works with the young child. The following quote by Rudolf Steiner about the nature of "gesture, in the widest sense," inspired me to elaborate on the means by which early childhood educators support the child's learning during the first seven years of life as a set of qualitative gestures.

> From the first to the seventh year, gesture predominates in the life of the young child, but gesture in the widest sense of the word, gesture that in the child lives in imitation.

Despite their Waldorf training, many teachers working in Waldorf classrooms may be unconsciously guided by what they met as children in their own education. Having resolved to better their own school experiences, they have decided to teach young human beings out of greater insight into the ways in which the child learns.

Yet breaking the patterns of what were most likely over-intellectualized practices in their own education requires ongoing consciousness of the deeper educational principles which guide the Waldorf teacher. It also asks the teachers to think in a new

81

way about what stands behind the topic they are presenting. This can be thought of as the artistic approach, in part because it does not involve a straight line from the immediate goal (e.g., learning to read) to a deeper one (e.g., the role of reading in opening countless worlds). In addition, an artist is able to see and present things which often do not occur to the casual observer.

As many of us can attest, the feelings of engagement and even enthusiasm when we encounter an artistic presentation are also present in good teaching. Such presentations awaken us to new facets of what might otherwise seem ordinary and uninteresting. If you teach astronomy, for instance, you want to take your students outside to observe the sky. Many of them will be awestruck by the vastness and beauty of the dome of the heavens on a clear, dark night. But if you want them to see and identify not only the constellations, but the apparent permanence of the fixed stars, you must prepare them to "see" before they are swept up in the immediate experience. Then you can speak of how the Ancient Greeks, like all human beings from time immemorial, saw a reflection of the human condition in the sky, and how they learned about themselves from these cosmic images. So it was that many millennia ago, the inhabitants of Greece identified the constellation Cassiopeia as the throne of the vain queen who bragged that she was more beautiful than the sea nymphs. She was punished by being cast into the sky where she perpetually wheels around the North Star. This story not only helps students to remember this constellation, but can also lead to a conversation in the class about how a preoccupation with superficial qualities weakens one's focus on the things in life which matter. Of course, one can find other qualities on which to focus within the scope of teaching astronomy. That is what makes the work of the individual Waldorf teachers so central to this education.

Central to the artistic presentation of material is the use of images. As the example of Cassiopeia above suggests, a story that brings the child to vivid inner pictures is a powerful incentive to observe and consider the subject at hand. The influence of images as generators of interest and enthusiasm stands in sharp contrast to the ossifying influence of rigidly defined concepts. The human mind yearns for stories, for inner pictures that stir the soul and awaken strong feelings. A child who is told to memorize that "Cassiopeia rotates around the North Star counter-clockwise" in order to give the correct answer on a test will, in all likelihood, forget this factoid as soon as the test is over. Nothing of any significance will remain in that child's mind. In contrast, even if the geometrical facts themselves recede from consciousness, the child who pictured the story of the vain queen will have built a relationship of curiosity and engagement with the surrounding universe. That relationship is a gift that does not disappear.

Furthermore, as anyone knows who has observed an artistic creation, the meaning and the understanding of that work can change over time. This is also the case with the inner image which is evoked in the child by the teacher's artistic presentation. The understanding which is derived from and associated with this image will grow with the young person, potentially providing an expanding and never-ending source of knowledge whenever the image is revisited.

Work in the high school asks more of the students in terms of bringing conscious observation to what they do. But here, we resist the temptation to explain the theory and instead lead the students to discover what the all-embracing concept might be. Now, after first setting the context in which the object of study is placed, the students experience an activity which stimulates them to add first-hand experience to the preliminary understanding with which they began. The high school students are increasingly encouraged to examine a subject by bringing their own thinking to bear. Here, the feelings engendered by this kind of "primary research" activity enrich both the given and the emerging concepts. In this way, the students can begin to add their own experience to the intellectual construct they have been offered. The concepts so acquired can increasingly become their own creation rather than just acquired knowledge.

Thus, a ninth grade class in History through Drama might read and act out scenes from plays from many cultures and ages. Taking on parts and becoming those stage characters; looking at, building, and experiencing the costumes, properties, and scenery—all this gives the students a chance to feel for themselves something of the people of that time and place. From there, the students can begin to explore the consciousness and the contemporary world in which the people of that time lived.

Another methodological principle entails the principle of moving from the whole to the parts. Rudolf Steiner gave curricular and methodological indications aimed at countering the atomization of modern thought into ever-smaller bits of information. Such a collection of various facts, he indicated, would tell the human being less and less about our true nature and about their true place in the natural world. He urged teachers to recognize that the world and the human being have a wholeness to them which cannot be seen merely as the sum of their parts. No matter how much we analyze brain function to understand why a human being acts in a particular way, the human being cannot be understood without taking the whole being, physical, emotional and spiritual, into account. This includes not only the physical organs and forms of the human being, but those aspects whose workings are not to be seen. This is not merely a matter of psychology, but the posited reality of a spiritual side to the human being as well.

In teaching history or literature, then, Steiner asked the teachers to reckon with what came before in someone's biography or in their story as well as what came after (or is still in the process of becoming for people who are alive now). The whole span of a lifetime was to be considered, not just the notable moments. Likewise, he asked them to take in all the factors in a phenomenon whether in physics or the introduction of number. So, for instance, in teaching geometry in the elementary school, a teacher may begin by having the children stand and slowly turn in place so that the view constantly changes as they rotate through a full 360 degrees. They may then be asked to walk a straight line followed by the forms of regular polygons such as triangles and pentagons. Based on this experience the teacher may then ask how we measure the distance of a given line or at what angle do we go forward from our starting point before we turn. All of this leads to the construction of many geometrical forms, first in two dimensions on paper, later in three-dimensional solids, and in the high school to the study of projective geometry in which lines disappear and reappear through infinity.

Even the introduction of number in the first grade leads the child to experience the truth that the parts come from the whole. The young child can perceive how all numbers begin with one and that everything proceeds from there. From one stick, we can get two sticks if we break off a piece, then three pieces, and so on. In this way, one (1) is the biggest number, it is the "whole," while the other numbers are really "parts" or "sub-sections" of this "whole." This concept can grow with the child, contributing to a sense that the human being, too, is an indivisible whole whose many parts (body, soul, and spirit; thinking, feeling, and willing; brain, heart, and lungs, etc.) are all subsets of this whole.

Perhaps the most difficult aspect of the methodology to understand in the Waldorf approach to education is the importance of rhythm and repetition in learning. This notion is foundational to the way in which children are taught. The teacher resists the temptation to give the children too much information or too much of an experience in a given lesson or on a given day. He or she asks, "What is the most important point I want the children to take away from the lesson?" rather than focusing on the presentation of many facts. Teachers know that the child's ability to retain, understand, and enjoy a meaningful learning experience requires time to digest what has been encountered. This means that the teacher allows the children to sleep on what was taught and then revisits it by having the children draw it out of themselves by retelling what they heard and experienced. In taking an experience through sleep, they achieve a distance from it. This then gives them a chance to re-create (as does the "artist" noted above)—now partly out of themselves—what was previously presented. They work with these new concepts, coming to learn them ever more deeply out of repeated recreations. Repetition serves to solidify what they have helped to re-create.

This approach to teaching and learning has its own lawful rhythm: presenting something new on day one and then recalling and applying the material by repeating it on day two. There is then a kind of breathing which takes place, always putting the child's learning process into the middle:

» the teacher presents;
» the child recapitulates and re-creates the next day;
» the teacher and the child work with the material in a further repetition so that the child's will is engaged in an outwardly visible way.

The principles of Waldorf methodology are integral to its efficacy. But it bears repeating that the individual teacher needs to take up these methods and apply them out of his or her own genius, not simply copy what someone else has done before.

ENDNOTES

1   The term "artistic" does not necessarily mean the traditional arts (singing, drawing, sculpting, etc.), but rather that, like those arts, the perceptually manifest reveals something invisible through utilizing perceptible media. Thus a math problem or science project can be just as artistic as storytelling or painting.

2   This mirrors the development of human cognition, which is at first active in the limbs and only later in the head.

3   There are four basic rhythms with which the Waldorf teacher works. The most basic of those is the day-night (or two-day) rhythm. Material that is presented on a given day is allowed to "go to sleep" before it is reviewed and brought to conceptual clarity on the following day. A second rhythm is that of the week. It is "the interest rhythm" and teachers strive to complete an engagement with a topic within a week of working on it. A paper that is returned to the student after more than a week will no longer be interesting to the student. The only interesting thing will be the teacher's comments, but the topic itself is already past the "interest window." A third rhythm is that of four weeks. A block, or unit of instruction, is usually best covered in four-week periods. This life-rhythm can be understood in contemplation of feminine reproductive cycles, for example, and can be said to bring a topic to a temporary level of maturity. The last of the pedagogical rhythms is that of a year. This is the time it can take for a new concept to be mastered to the degree that it can be used as a capacity. Thus a mathematical concept introduced early in third grade should be mastered sufficiently to be assumed as a capacity for work at the beginning of fourth grade.

Two Contributions to the Study of the Sixth Core Principle

Core Principle 6 *Relationships*
Enduring human relationships between students and their teachers are essential and irreplaceable. The task of all teachers is to work with the developing individuality of each student and with each class as a whole. Truly human pedagogical relationships gain in depth and stability when they are cultivated over many years. They cannot be replaced by instruction utilizing computers or other electronic means. Healthy working relationships with parents and colleagues are also essential to the well-being of the class community and the school.

First Contribution

Judy Lucas

Rudolf Steiner delivered a series of lectures to members of the Anthroposophical Society during February and March of 1919, in the aftermath of the Great War, in an effort to bring order out of chaos.[1] In one of those lectures Rudolf Steiner boldly stated: "People hardly know what it means to be human." (p.2) Waldorf education was indeed founded with the intention of bringing social renewal and a new understanding of human existence and the social organism. At the core of this new social organism is the image of the human being (Core Principle #1) and the individual's relationship to other human beings (Core Principle #6). He addresses the development of a new kind of cognitive feeling and what it can generate in us:

> It is solely by means of this feeling that spiritual science can bring us to a proper appraisal of what a human being is, to a feeling for human dignity in the context of the world. This feeling can fill our whole soul, and only if it extends to every part of our inner being can it put us in the proper mood to sort out, if need be, our relationship to another person. We can regard this as one of the first substantial achievements of modern anthroposophically based spiritual science: a proper respect for the human element in the world. (p.3)

Steiner explains that in olden times our thoughts and actions were driven by spiritual leaders and that we were therefore joined in a spiritually-driven community. Now our thoughts and actions come largely out of our own individual freedom, thus necessarily separating us one from the other. Therefore, we must consciously direct ourselves to be in community, to cultivate human relationships.

One strategy Steiner gives us toward accomplishing this is to "recognize that divine activity is at work in our neighbor" (p.12) and that we can sharpen this recognition through a specific meditation. He suggests that we take moments to reflect upon our own lives, asking ourselves how this life of ours has unfolded since childhood, and noticing not so much what we ourselves have enjoyed and experienced, but rather:

> ...the people who have entered our lives as parents, brothers and sisters, friends, teachers and so on and,

in place of ourselves, focus our attention on the inner
nature of each of these people. After a while we shall
come to realize how little we actually owe to ourselves
and how much is due to all that has flowed into us
from others. (p.13)

And further:

If a person looks again and again into his own being
and recognizes the contribution which other people,
perhaps long dead, or who have ceased to be close
to him, have made to his life, his whole involvement
with other people will become such that on forming an
individual relationship with someone, an imagination
of the true being of this person will arise within him.
(p.13)

Steiner ends the lecture with a suggestion that the best
situation arises when we learn from each other, especially inter-
generationally. The youth can know that all stages of life hold
treasures—perhaps a necessary, comforting thought at times—
and the elders can be inspired by the youth. The class teacher's
commitment to work with a group of students over eight years
and the enduring human relationship between a class of students
and their class teacher allow for an evolving, inter-generational
collective learning. When we are honest, we have to recognize
that no one individual can be an expert in all of the curriculum
areas covered during these eight years. Therefore, the opportunity
Waldorf education provides for a teacher to stay with the class
over this period of time (when possible) places a value on
relationship over curriculum content. In fact, this Core Principle
was inspired by Jørgen Smit's lecture, in which he spoke about the
"general stream" (the curriculum taught to everyone in the class)

and the "individual stream" of relationships with each student.[2] It is the seeing of the individual child that needs the ripening of several years, as mentioned in the body of the principle. There is an impulse for social renewal underlying Waldorf pedagogy, and this impulse can be realized only by attending to each individual as well as to the class as a whole, which can also mean the nurturing of the student-to-student relationships. This level of instruction cannot be replaced by computer instruction or other electronic means. This is what it means to be human.

For me, this is essential. In fact, one of my life's commitments is to try to have an imagination of the true being of the "other," of the people with whom I interact daily. In the context of education, the teacher leads the students in a process whereby they learn to bracket their own interests and identity long enough to perceive and even appreciate the interests and identities of others. We develop the students' critical thinking to allow them to utterly open themselves to the views and needs of other human beings. By creating opportunities for students to examine their own generally unexamined assumptions, biases, and prejudices, we allow students to explore the perhaps unexamined assumptions, biases, and prejudices of others. We can then push the critical thinking, through an analytical process, to enter the realm of empathy. Students can learn to experience the feelings of other human beings; they learn to empathize.

Carl Rogers, one of the founders of the humanistic approach to psychology, identified three conditions necessary for therapeutic change: empathy, unconditional positive regard for the other, and the communication of both to the other. I suggest that we must go beyond the recognition of the importance of human relationship in education toward a conscious cultivation of our human relationships, a cultivation that includes empathy and an unconditional positive regard for the other. Steiner says, "The kind of relationship there is between one person and another, this kind of interest in things, this conscious participation in life, will be there as a matter of course in an independent organism that is on its way to becoming sound." (p.43) A school as organism, a faculty council, even education itself, is sound inasmuch as the people involved cultivate an interest in one another.

Leading Thoughts

When I was asked to write an article on this Core Principle, I was struck by my own need for human relationships as a way to understand the need for human relationships more generally. The Pedagogical Section Council does not intend for these Core Principles to be pedantic or prescriptive, but rather to be inspiring, to be leading thoughts for dynamic conversations on what is essential in Waldorf education and to stimulate different interpretations and perspectives. Therefore, I felt the necessity to engage in my own conversations around this specific Core Principle. What follows are some leading thoughts from my community of relationships. This first quote is from a Waldorf parent:

> At one level, relationship in Waldorf education is a spiritual commitment, a recognition of the essential value and divinity of every single person. At a second, it is an ethical commitment to honoring each individual's right of self-determination, combined with responsibility to the collective well-being. And at a third level, that of society, it is that responsibility to respect all of other human beings, to embrace diversity and difference of all kinds, and to work toward the good of the community and the world, in engaged citizenship. Thus relationship is at once spiritual, ethical, and social. In the realm of education, it is

preparation of Waldorf students with very real-world dispositions and skills: the ability to think critically about different perspectives, including one's own; the ability to work with others, all others, in teamwork situations; the ability to solve complex real-world problems, all of which include human relationship; and the ability to think and act inclusively, which is an essential skill in a global world.

A colleague of mine, a teacher at the Denver Waldorf School, spoke of his own curiosity to understand the people behind world events and to shed light on these individuals in his classes. Who was Rosa Parks? Why did she refuse to surrender her seat to a white person? Was this an impulse of the moment, or the consequence of fatigue, or a well-laid plan? My colleague asks me, when we say, "The South segregated black people," who do we mean by "the South"? When we look at an atomic clock and try to understand how it works, can we also try to understand a little about Isidor Rabi, a physics professor at Columbia University, who suggested that a clock could be made from a technique he developed in the 1930s called atomic beam magnetic resonance?

When visiting a sister Waldorf school on behalf of the Pedagogical Section Council, I guided the staff and then the board members in a collaborative discussion on the Core Principles. They have continued to study together these core principles, since my visit, as a school community. Here are some of the comments that I have heard from these groups:

» The position of teachers, having authority and guidance, is all too often taken away by the use of technology.
» Important in our Waldorf schools is the human relationships of class teachers to subject teachers as they work together to meet the needs of the children.

» We bring depth to our teaching when we do a child study as a faculty, and we can then place the child within a whole context.

» Human relationships create possibilities for children to take risks.

» We as teachers and staff must invest in relationships with parents, establish an open rapport, provide a picture of what's happening in class with their children.

» This principle is what brought us to the school.

» Our roles as teachers, parents, and board members are really to model healthy relationships and communication and how to work through conflict in a positive and respectful way.

» Our graduates are good at, and open to, relationships.

In my inquiry into how others perceive the importance of human relationship to Waldorf education, I came across an article by Craig Holdrege entitled "Reality-Based Education in a Hyper-real Culture"[3] in which he talks about "commanding presences," a term coined by Albert Borgmann. In his article, Holdrege talks of commanding or genuine presences "as characterizing the real— when you perceive that something is rooted in a larger context of which it is revelatory." He gives an example: "A leaf in the fall, loosed from its tree and floating through the air, is revelatory of the whole context of wind and temperature at that moment." He goes on to raise the question:

> ... how do we orchestrate or facilitate experiences with commanding presences today for children in education? Because we all know and perceive how today, from an early age on, the experience of children is often mediated through so many gadgets and devices. We

really need to concentrate, then, on how we can help children still come into contact with commanding presences. How could we make that the main focus of their existence for the first 10 or 12 years of their lives?

It would mean that school would have to become very different in our technological age and less what we typically imagine school to be. Tests would have to go away; 45-minute periods would have to go away. Meeting with people, meeting with nature, meeting through meaningful work in the world, such as gardening—all of that would become the heart of education.

Why? Because the commanding presences give us roots in the world and help form the way we think about the world. They are in the best sense of the word formative and can inform our being. If there is to be a future in which human beings form ideas that are rooted in reality, it will be in part because they've been allowed to participate in commanding presences as children. And they will have experienced that reality is relational, that as a person you are active and you are being acted upon by commanding presences.

"Have Courage for the Truth"

Steiner, in the lecture cycle mentioned repeatedly, developed an understanding of what he called the Threefold Social Organism. He began the lecture by explaining that "it is people's soul needs which cause them to seek each other out, and it is these similar soul needs which unite them. Education, too, means that one person cares for another in the realm of the inner life." (pp.45–46) And then:

What human beings shall gradually acquire through working with spiritual science [for instance, in Waldorf education] is an awareness that every human

relationship is inwardly related to the whole of
humanity and to the wider world. (p.54)

Steiner then described that in our striving toward human
collaboration, we can find two different paths, the thinking path
and the willing path, both of which are important as we engage
socially. We can find our way to human collaboration through a
thinking path in this way:

> We must strive for the mental honesty—pluck up the
> courage to be able to admit it, in utter sincerity, that...
> we are not born free from prejudice where our world
> of thought is concerned; we are all born with certain
> prejudices. (p.59)

He goes on to explain that, though we are born with
prejudices, we can become reborn out of the thoughts of others
with a comprehensive feeling in our own thoughts. We can choose
to embrace a collective thinking. He adds, "It must become a
serious part of our lives to educate ourselves to acquire a sense
for considering other people's thoughts, and to correct bias in
ourselves through conversations with others." (p.63) When I can
stop thinking that I myself am the sole source of everything I
think and recognize in my innermost soul, that I am a part of
humanity, then I have found the path to human collaboration.

When we bridle our impulse to share our own thoughts in a
faculty council and instead take a moment to listen deeply to what
is being said by others, when we begin a meeting with parents
by allowing them to speak from their hearts while we listen to
them with deep concern and interest, when we work with our
colleagues to build a picture of the child from many perspectives,
when we allow a high school student to lead a review or present
new material in class, then we are truly able to "inquire into the

path of thought which consists in acquiring tolerance of mind for the opinions of mankind in general, and developing a social interest in the thoughts of others." (p.63) We can model this state of mind and heart for our students, leading them in their own interactions to the thought that it is not only acceptable for them to have different opinions, but desirable. As an administrator I came to love the ability within a Waldorf setting to allow for social conflict, to allow students a chance to become really angry. I was challenged to normalize, not remove, conflict. Yes, when the conflict becomes severe, it is the task of the adults to intervene, but not with the intention of ending conflict. Instead, the task is to allow the students to express their differences in a heartfelt manner, then to ponder the differences of opinions, then to value those differences. In this way, we lead the students toward a connection to the other, toward an overcoming of individual bias, toward a healthy social organism, out of the "chaos of war" in which they are living.

On other occasions, when high school students would come to me enraged over a rule they felt to be arbitrary, I felt challenged to understand how they felt about the rule, why they did not understand it or feel they could abide by it. And through an understanding of the students' perspective, I could then either explain the rule in a way that would make sense to them and therefore allow a conformity to the rule, or go back to the high school teachers and advocate for a process to either remove the rule or modify it.

"Imbue Thyself with the Power of Imagination"

A second way to the human collaboration is through willing, which Steiner described as an acquired idealism and enthusiasm, or the ability

...to acquire the kind of idealism that does not spring merely from the blood and youthful enthusiasm, but is acquired out of our own initiative...the kind which springs from taking hold of the life of the spirit, and which can be rekindled afresh again and again because we have made it part of our soul independently of our bodily existence. (p.63)

When we offer fairy tales and Aesop's fables without the moral, but simply allowing the students to live deeply with awe into the magic of the story, then we are educating them toward an acquired idealism and enthusiasm. In the grades, when children begin to learn the laws of mathematics, the orderliness and beauty of multiplication leading into geometry, the enduring truths of mathematics, they are filled with an imagination of the infinite, which they will later explore further in projective geometry. When we allow the students to discover what happens when an electric current passes through a coil rather than tell them first and only demonstrate it as evidence for the theory, students uncover for themselves an abiding belief in truth.

If you inquire into the path of the will, you will not hear of something abstract but of the need to educate yourself in idealism. And if you cultivate this idealism or, which is particularly necessary, you introduce it into the education of growing children, a sense will awaken for acting out of the spirit; out of this idealism will come impulses to do more than one is pushed into doing from outside. (p.63)

"Sharpen Thy Feeling for Responsibility of Soul"

And now we can find a third path, through feeling, through a sensing of what is needed. Out of this idealism will come impulses to do more than one is pushed into doing from outside oneself.

When the teacher guides the students, through relationship, to recognize their biases and begin to shed them and to acquire idealism through the uncovering of truth and beauty, the students can begin to recognize the need to become active members of a growing healthy social organism and to be responsible for the development of this same organism.

> Out of a thinking which is intrinsically tolerant and interested in the thoughts of others, and out of a will reborn through acquiring idealism, something arises that cannot be called anything else but a heightened feeling of responsibility for everything you do. (p.65)

In a Waldorf school, we teach reading, writing, and arithmetic, but we use these three Rs as tools to uncover three more essential Rs: rhythm, ritual, and reverence. Through the rhythm and cadences of iambic pentameter in recited verses, or the bouncing of the ball to the times tables, or the daily, weekly, seasonal, and yearly rhythms we establish, and through the observation of these natural rhythms, we allow our students to see themselves integrally connected to the world of nature around them. "Everything that speaks to us from the various kingdoms of nature, if we contemplate all this in the light of anthroposophically based spiritual science, we find that in one way or another it is connected with the human being." (p.4) The establishment of ritual in a classroom, the speaking of a morning verse followed by birthday verses and an exercise in eurythmy, for example, establishes the student in relationship to the class of students. Through an understanding of the student as a human being and a further understanding of students in relation to others in a classroom and a ritualistic order defining these relationships, we enable students to "attain a living relationship between ourselves as human beings and the whole of the rest of the world." (p.5) And through deeply-rooted rhythms and carefully established social rituals, students are led to an idealistic enthusiasm for the divine, a reverence for the mystery, and a "direct presence of the spirit, the active power of the spirit." (p.5) In the words of Emerson, "Every spirit builds itself a house; and beyond its house, a world; and beyond its world, a heaven. Know then, that the world exists for you: build therefore, your own world."

The world that Steiner invites us to fashion is intended to create true spiritual harmony, real spiritual collaboration. This world can in fact be an ordering of our current chaos. "We must not take an exclusively pessimistic view of the present time; we can also draw from it the strength to achieve a kind of vindication of contemporary existence." (p.89) This world is not possible without humans in relationship with one another. While the metaphor of a chain-link fence may seem overused, it is in fact an essential picture of social harmony. Each link in the chain must have its own individual integrity, and the integrity of the chain is dependent on each of the links. Likewise, each link, no matter how strong, cannot fulfill the intention of a chain without being linked to the others. As educators we need to respond "to the clear pointer calling us to play our part in social healing." (p.89) This is done through human relationship. I end with our well-loved verse:

> The healing social life is found only
> When, in the mirror of each soul,
> The whole community finds its reflection,
> And when, in the whole community,
> The virtue of each one is living.

ENDNOTES

1   Rudolf Steiner, *The Esoteric Aspect of the Social Question* (London: Rudolf Steiner Press, 2001).

2   Jørgen Smit, *The Child, the Teachers, and the Community*, lecture 2 (Spring Valley: Mercury Press, 1992).

3   Craig Holdrege, *Reality-Based Education in a Hyper-real Culture*, available at: natureinstitute.org/txt/ch/techno-utopia.htm

Second Contribution

James Pewtherer

As insightful as is the curriculum which Rudolf Steiner and the teachers developed in the first Waldorf School, it would have had little value if there were not dedicated teachers bringing it to life for those first children in the school. For a Waldorf teacher's primary job is not only to teach children to love learning and to introduce them to the richness of the world, but it is also to so educate the children and students that they can grow into full human beings. It is for this reason that Steiner also recognized that it was crucial that the children and teachers build class communities in which mutual love among them would grow out of warm interest in all that went on in each of those classrooms. Out of the trust which was then developed between teacher and children and among the children themselves, the teacher could help each child grow to know him- or herself, that is, to become a self-educator. A central task of education, in Steiner's view, is to remove the obstacles which stand in the way of a young human being's discovery of his or her true individual tasks in life. To achieve this, the teacher is obliged to develop intimate knowledge of each student and to work with each unique being. Along with this gentle, loving guidance, the teacher is to lead the children to learn about and to love the world around them with a love that will continue to grow for their lifetime. This is a work which no machine can do. For as marvelous a tool as a computer is, it is no substitute for the complex tasks which a true teacher undertakes.

Instead, internet technology is well-suited for such undertakings as accruing facts and compiling lists of such things as formulae, tasks which are well-suited to the binary system underlying internet technology. But the complexity which is a human being cannot be reduced to the point that it can be properly met by an algorithm, no matter how sophisticated. Many "educational" software programs exist which can help to organize facts, explain mathematical processes, provide lists of spelling words, and have children practice their skills. But at the end of the day, a teacher is needed to seize the unique moment with *this* particular class, on *this* particular day, to expand on *this* particular question from a child in the context, for instance, of that child's struggle over many weeks. In spite of the business plans of some technology companies to develop curricular software that would have teachers reduced to being clerks who implement identical pre-packaged curricula in every school across the land, the real teacher will win out every time. For it is the teacher's intimate knowledge of the child and the child's deep love for his teacher that is the basis for true education.

So it is that the world over, six-year-old first graders look up to the teacher as *the* model in their lives. This revered person even supplants the parents in some ways in the mind of the child as the one who knows how the world works. The children invest their teacher with near-mythical powers when it comes to doing the things that happen in school. "Ms. Jones is the *best* artist, the *best* singer, the *best* story-teller..." and so forth. They have complete faith that she will be there loving them and helping them to learn everything there is to know and do in the world. And the trust in their teacher that is established in these first years of schooling will serve as the rock upon which they will build their confidence in her guidance, demands, and expectations of them in sixth, seventh, and eighth grades.

When the class teacher (and also subject teachers who devote themselves to a class over years) demonstrates to the child a deep confidence in and loving knowledge of that child, the foundation for an abiding trust in the world is established for life. The child must have the feeling of being known so well by the teacher that this revered figure will not allow him to be less than is possible. Of course, what the child is capable of on a given day can vary somewhat based on levels of fatigue or health or other outer factors. The teacher, then, needs to have a sense of the range of ability of the child overall so as to judge what is possible in that moment. At the same time, the wise teacher inculcates the expectation that one's sense of dedication to the work will also be a strong incentive to rise to the occasion no matter one's mood. With the teacher's wise guidance, each child must learn over time to be self-aware, to know whether enough hard and wholesome work has been done so as to put beautiful and thoughtful work into the world. The important thing along the way is that, responding out of the love and authority of the teacher, the child feels deep down, "My teacher knows what is best for me right now, even if I don't want to do it." Even when the child's resistance is overruled in that moment, that underlying confidence is there. This means that it will also be incumbent on me as teacher to know what support the child needs at that moment, whether in academic, practical, or artistic work in the class. This determination also needs to be augmented by a fine sense for the feeling and will life of the child.

When the children gradually grow to become youths in the later elementary years and into high school, the habits and values that they have membered into their souls in the early years increasingly become their own, but now in a more conscious way. The single class teacher and the elementary school subject teachers are now replaced by a circle of high school teachers, experts in their own fields, who now draw out of the students what was cultivated in their less-rigorous thinking life and in their childlike feeling life in earlier years. They converse with their teachers and classmates, examining their inchoate and often unarticulated thoughts from within, learning to develop these thoughts in a way that they can bring them into expression. In addition to this gradual awakening at the hand of the high school faculty, each student needs at least one dedicated teacher (often called an advisor) who makes it his/her special task to meet with the student and gently inquire as to how each is doing. Here again, the deft teacher puts the right questions at the right time, allowing the adolescent the room to open his/her deepest thoughts to the teacher if the time is right. Creating intimate and safe places in which to explore a teenager's inner questions can also help to cultivate the student's own developing powers of reason.

Throughout the grades, the teacher develops curriculum and lesson plans that will meet the children as an entire class community in terms of their studies and in what is of particular import at that point in time. Rudolf Steiner's curriculum indications were predicated on the thought that each teacher's understanding of human development would guide him/her in finding the topics, approaches, and activities which would guide the educational choices made for the class. Here, then, the regular and ongoing study of *The Foundations of Human Experience/ Study of Man* and the other educational and anthroposophic courses which Rudolf Steiner gave is essential. The levels of complexity in the human being and in human development call for lifetimes of study. Just to understand such concepts as the activity of soul, spirit, and body obliges us to ponder Steiner's explications again and again. But at the end of the day, it is only out of our understanding of who the child is at any age, be it 4, 9, or 16, for instance, that we can claim to be good teachers for the particular group of children or young people before us.

We can now turn from our consideration of the teacher's relationship to the destinies of individual children, including the preparation for prospective individual life tasks, and look at the surrounding class community. Here, an apparently random group of children comes together and forms a cohort which will be together for as many as 12 or 14 years. The gender balance, the relative youth or maturity of the group within its grade, the balance of temperaments, the bonds between particular children—all these contribute to what a particular class will be known for over the years. This class becomes a kind of home for the children in which they and their peers will learn such things as kindness, caring, dispute resolution, working together for the good of the whole, helping others, and being helped by them. They also will learn to work hard, to share common tasks, to have each one do his/her share as a member of the community, and to listen to other points of view. These and many other life lessons are taken in by learning together in a community.

In this constellation, the child can feel him- or herself surrounded by an entire group who are rather like siblings. The give-and-take of living together; of rubbing off each other's "sharp corners"; of learning to appreciate the differences between us; of subjugating my wishes for the good of the group; of taking up leadership when it is needed; of standing up for "what is right" when others don't necessarily see it—all these lessons and many more are part of the reality of the class community which is a central element of Waldorf education. Here again, the teacher or teachers are ones who are crucial to guiding this important process. The teachers need to have enough self-knowledge to know when to consciously guide the community and when to stand back and allow the students to learn as they develop their own social processes.

One of the most telling of Rudolf Steiner's remarks to the teachers in terms of their relationships came at the end of a faculty meeting in Stuttgart on September 26, 1919. "The vital thing is that there is always contact, and that teachers and pupils form a unity."[3] Being together in a healthy way with their class really means giving the students another home.

In addition to the focus on the children, the teachers in a Waldorf school must also turn their attention, as far as human relationships are concerned, to the relationship with other adults. Without these other relationships, this sacred task of truly educating children cannot be achieved. Beyond the primary relationship with the children and students, teachers will be successful educators only if they also develop healthy relationships with colleagues, parents, administrative staff, and beyond. In all these relationships, different social skills are needed, for in the work with ego-endowed adults, the teacher needs to build partnerships based on equality.

Our interactions with teaching colleagues are an ever-present model for our students. The very considerations and skills which we seek to cultivate in the children are also demanded of us. This entails seeking the views of others, especially when an action or policy will affect other classes or the school as a whole. When we become teachers in a Waldorf school, we give up a certain amount of independence, but we do so with the knowledge that our colleagues can provide us with important insights that we might not have. Done well, making decisions as a conscious and responsible group leads to actions based on insight. At the same time, we all know how cumbersome the process of getting to a decision can be for a circle of colleagues in a Waldorf school. Yet our task of learning to steer the school is very much an important process in itself. Rudolf Steiner's clear admonition that the Waldorf school would be run in a republican manner instead of with a principal or headmaster makes our work clear. Taking the time to counsel each other is also part of the teacher's task.

Perhaps the most challenging part of the teacher's more outward-looking tasks is the cultivation of the work with the parents of the children in his/her care. These children have come to them from the world of spirit, and it is they who must feel the teacher to be a trusted partner. If that is there, the teacher can participate in the child's upbringing, making the education as effective as it can be. The Waldorf teacher is in a unique position in the experience of most parents. For in the Waldorf school over eight years, the teacher develops an intimate knowledge of the child. Unlike the parents' relationship, the teacher's relationship comes without being related to the child by blood. Accordingly, the teacher can have more of an objective distance from the child and can see some things about him/her more clearly than can the parents. Yet perceptive parents can have intuitive and experiential knowledge of the child which is invaluable for the teacher's understanding. Thus, the better the teacher can listen to the parents' observations and experience and also clearly communicate the "what" and the "how" of the approach she/he is taking to meet the needs of the child, the more powerful will be the partnership on behalf of the child.

Turning to another area of relationships, we can recognize that the administrative burdens of 21st century schooling and the effective operation of a school-organism have become more complicated. These tasks can be greatly aided when there are administrators and office staff who collaborate with the faculty to execute required expectations. Here, too, it is the teachers who must take the lead in making sure that administrative forms and tasks in the school are structured so as to benefit the children. Yet sharing the imaginations and inspirations which inform the teaching work while at the same time eliciting, listening to and learning from the observations of administrative staff can also serve the children. So, too, where there is a board of directors, who, in safeguarding the operation and financial health of the school, can also provide very helpful support, the faculty has a strong ally in meeting its tasks.

Perhaps of greatest importance in our work with the children, insofar as it is in the realm of human relationships, is the need to reckon with and work with the spiritual beings in whose name we teach. Rudolf Steiner put this need to the first teachers at the very beginning of the *Study of Man* introductory course on the evening before it began, August 21, 1919. He told the gathered teachers that "...we first try to be conscious of the links which we want to forge with the spiritual worlds... [and of the charge] to be aware of the need to create contacts with the spiritual powers at whose behest and under whose mandate each one of us will have to work." Steiner evoked the names of the Third Hierarchy—Angels, Archangels and Archai—again and again in his lectures about the education: These beings are the sources of our Imaginations, Inspirations and Intuitions respectively, and it is these gifts which make our work with other human beings successful. These beings, however, leave us free; it is completely up to us whether or not we develop an inner relationship with them. This relationship depends upon what he called the only truly free deed of which we are capable as inhabitants of the earthly world, that is, choosing to be meditants.

Rudolf Steiner implied the relationship with the gods when he spoke about the relationship with people: "In the evenings before your meditation, ask the Angels, Archangels, and Archai that they may help you in your work on the following day. In the mornings, after the meditation, you may feel yourself united with the beings of the Third Hierarchy."

And perhaps the most powerful picture of all of relationships is the picture Rudolf Steiner gave to the first teachers on that first evening as to how they would work together in what is known as the *College Imagination*. He portrayed the gathered teachers as having spiritual beings behind them and above them, and as contributing gifts of light to the circle they form when they are meeting together. Here then, the matter of relationships broadens and deepens to include beings from the non-physical world.

When we can enrich our human relationships with some of those elements referenced in this article, we will find that we have the strength, the courage, and (sometimes!) the wisdom to educate the children so that they can become healthy human beings.

Two Contributions to the Study of the Seventh Core Principle

CORE PRINCIPLE *7 Spiritual Orientation*
In order to cultivate the imaginations, inspirations, and intuitions needed for their work, Rudolf Steiner gave the teachers an abundance of guidance for developing an inner, meditative life. This guidance includes individual professional meditations and an imagination of the circle of teachers forming an organ of spiritual perception. Faculty and individual study, artistic activity, and research form additional facets of ongoing professional development.

First Contribution
Introduction
Elan Leibner

After studying the image of the human being, the phases of child development, the notion of a developmentally appropriate curriculum, the challenge of freedom in teaching, and the methodological principles (CPs 1–5), the Core Principles take a turn from the general, universal aspects of education. The challenge of relationships (#6) is always a specific one. A teacher has to develop a relationship with a child, or a group of children, or a whole class, and with colleagues and parents, but it is always a specific situation between specific human beings. There are no general solutions to individual challenges in relationships, although, of course, there are principles that one can apply. When all of the low-hanging fruits of problem-solving have been picked, there is a layer of the soul that cannot be reached through technique and advice from without. An honest contemplation of the issues that arise through relationships with students, fellow teachers, administrators, and parents points toward mysteries that are not accessible intellectually. These mysteries are not unique to school situations; parenting, marriage, and many other human relationships similarly point toward an ineffable core that must be reached in depths to which the intellect has no access.

The moment one becomes aware of these mysteries, the whole path we have followed so far, from the image of the human being on, points the way toward levels of knowing that are not informational alone. A task is thereby indicated: to cultivate a way of knowing that places oneself face to face with the invisible realities of life. Thus we arrive at meditation.

Rudolf Steiner indicated at least three levels of knowing above the intellectual: Imaginative, Inspirational, and Intuitive. In books, lectures, and seminars, he ever and again tried to teach others how to become knowers of the invisible. He even told the teachers that it was a requisite aspect of their task that "in the field of education, we come to **an actual experience of the spiritual.**"[1] (emphasis mine)

This *actual experience of the spiritual* indicates a level of perception that transcends a mere intellectual study of anthroposophy. The teachers to whom Steiner was speaking were very familiar with his teachings; there was no need to introduce them to the concepts of spiritual realities and exercises. But Steiner wanted them to practice meditation and to achieve a degree of perception that, while perhaps not a full spiritual-research capacity, would nevertheless allow them to see their students with a level of comprehension that would open the door to innovative and healing directions. It is a daunting charge, to be sure. But the whole context of that statement, coming as it did in Steiner's last day of lecturing to the first Waldorf teachers (before his death) is clear indication that he considered what had been achieved to that point to be short of Waldorf education's potential. Spiritual orientation as a **practice** was absolutely necessary.

Already at the inception of the first Waldorf School, the teachers received both a professional meditation for individual practice and an imagination for cultivating a collective capacity for spiritual perception. These are usually called the *First Teachers' Meditation* and the *College Imagination*,[2] respectively. After the aforementioned lectures of 1923, Steiner gave them a second individual meditation.[3] These individual and group meditations make it clear that, like other worldly endeavors inspired by anthroposophy, education was conceived by Rudolf Steiner as a path of initiation. I would argue that the entire edifice of Waldorf education rests on the assumption of the teacher as a spiritual practitioner, and that without this assumption becoming a reality there is an active absence at the center of the endeavor.

A spiritual orientation is also more than just a meditative path. By "spiritual" Steiner meant something open-ended, without limits as far as growth and knowledge are concerned. Only the past is circumscribed for a human being, and the more we broaden our knowledge, open our hearts, and enlarge the scope of our activity, the fuller are we justified in being called human beings. Hence even more common efforts to develop professionally, such as faculty studies, refresher courses, and research projects, can come under the umbrella of a spiritual orientation.

ENDNOTES

1   Steiner, Rudolf. CW 302a, Lecture of October 16, 1923, published
     most recently in *Balance in Teaching*. Great Barrington, MA:
     SteinerBooks, 2007

2   See articles by Roberto Trostli in *Research Bulletin for Waldorf
     Education* Vol.16 No.2 and Vol.17 No.1. Also available in
     Creating a Circle of Collaborative Spiritual Leadership. Chatham,
     NY: Waldorf Publications, 2015.

3   See an article by the author in *Research Bulletin for Waldorf
     Education*, Vol.19 No.1 for a discussion of the difference between
     these two professional meditations.

Second Contribution

Frances Vig

As part of my work in the Chicago Waldorf high school, I teach
the history of architecture in 12th grade. Although I revise my
approach each year according to the class I will be teaching, in
recent years I have consistently opened the block by asking the
students to look at our rented school building from a different
perspective. By examining the physical structure and thinking
about the design process, they are asked to consider what ideas
the architect had about the human beings who would work in
that space and the children who would receive their education
there.

As the students consider each room and the connecting
corridors and stairways, the thinking behind the design of this
particular building becomes increasingly apparent. The architect
was bodying forth the ideas about children and their education
that the community held at that time. The students quickly discern
that the ideas behind Waldorf education are quite different and
that, ideally, the structure housing it requires a different form.

They come to realize that we are surrounded by the results of people's ideas expressed as materialized thoughts, whether in the visible design of homes, factories, hospitals, and prisons or the invisible structure of laws, regulations, and conventions. It is a small step for them to consider which ideas about the nature of the human being are implicit in both the visible and invisible spaces that we create and what their effects are on us.

The thought that these materialized forms are shaped by other human beings working within a specific context gives us the possibility to make changes out of our own context. As you can imagine, this possibility dramatically affects the quality of our class discussions. Exercising the ability to "read" the consciousness expressed through the architecture of the past and appreciating our inheritance become part of the journey the students experience, but what often intrigues them most is to look at current issues in the world and to find out how social change can be affected by the quality of the spaces we create. How are human beings responding to their surroundings in our time? The intentions that shape design become the focus of discussion and lead the students to think about the needs of the future they are approaching. How will they respond?

In the final block of 12th grade, we pick up this theme again when the students have an opportunity to review their education. They re-member their experiences by drawing images arising from their early childhood and from key moments in grade school. Looking at the murals they have created encourages all sorts of anecdotes and memories to surface. The ensuing discussions between those who have been in the school since the parent-tot stage and those who arrived later are richly peppered with stories—some of them funny, others sad—that reveal just how much children notice about their surroundings: details of the physical space, but also details of the soul space. These memories and the sharing of experiences, combined with time spent in early childhood and grade school classes, provoke many questions that become the content of the block.

Each year the intention behind the shaping of our school, as a faculty of teachers and administrative staff, becomes tangible in the questions and comments of the students. It is not always as delightful as we might wish. They have been educated to be perceptive, thoughtful, and articulate—and they are. It's interesting to hear what they have observed and what they think. I often feel that I am seeing their soul experience of what we as a faculty have formed out of our individual commitment and collective collaboration. What is this commitment? And what is the foundation for our collaborative research? How might we be different from any other intentional community with a common vision?

I am reminded of an anecdote told to me by a parent some years ago prior to the opening of our high school. Her son was a delightfully challenging student in the grade school, skilled in asking provocative questions and keeping us on our toes. A few years after leaving the grade school, he was discussing his future with his mother. When she asked what he wanted to do after college, he responded, "I don't know what I want to do, but I do know what I want to be. I want to *be* successful." When asked what success meant, his response was, "I want to be successful like the Waldorf teachers. They are all really different from one another, but they figure out how to get along and work together for us. There's something they have, but I don't know what it is." As his teachers we were, to say the least, rather astonished, delighted, and intrigued to hear this comment, as was his mother! What does this point to?

I think he was sensing the emerging intentional community that develops through the individual meditative practice of the colleagues, the forming and working out of shared agreements, shared study and artistic practice, ongoing professional development, all in a context of the power of an awakening love for the incarnating human being.

When I consider the comments of students, my thoughts turn to what is called the College Imagination. I am mindful of the fact that all the members of a faculty—teachers and administrative staff alike—can be engaged in the activity described in this imagination. The picture of adults' forming a chalice out of the power of their individual meditative striving, of the cup being woven out of a selfless sharing of each one's strengths and the heightened awareness that can allow a different quality of insight, is potent. I see the question of spiritual orientation as an essential element in the strengthening of the "vessel activity" that can generate the imaginations, inspirations, and intuitions needed for the work. Surely the question is not a simple *if* but *how* we participate in this work together. Roberto Trostli's article in the PSC publication, *Creating a Circle of Collaborative Spiritual Leadership*, addresses the work that can arise when this imagination is active in a school. [This article is also available in two parts in the *Research Bulletin*, vol.16 #2, and vol.17 #1 – Ed.]

From a soul perspective both teaching and parenting are "athletic" activities. One parent, at the end of the 12th grade year, described the experience as a certain culmination of a personal Long March, and he expressed a deep appreciation for the experience of working for fourteen years with the changing constellation of teachers. Looking back, he could see how the content of the curriculum and the style of approach taken by the teachers had an emerging coherence full of meaning for students and parents alike.

Despite the discussions we have about the right language for communicating Waldorf education, I think that the most effective language in any human encounter is that which arises when we are actively present, exercising a profound listening, and speaking out of our experience and understanding. It seems to me that we are effective to the degree that we understand the work of our colleagues in different subjects and levels and the role that they play in engaging the developmental curriculum. I think that we will find the language we need in each encounter when, as colleagues, we actively and authentically awaken the process of becoming a Waldorf school.

As teachers and administrators we know that what we do and how we work together is highly formative. When we take a position as teachers in a Waldorf school we are making a professional commitment that asks us to develop beyond our own personal inclinations without relinquishing our integrity. In the first lecture of *Study of Man* (CW 293), Rudolf Steiner speaks of the deep relationship that forms between teacher and students when that teacher concerns herself with thoughts about the spiritual nature of the evolving human being. This relationship also has the effect of helping us overcome our own individual one-sidedness and personal inclinations and encourages us to be more aware and attentive.

While Steiner is focused here on the student-teacher relationships, this also has a profound effect on all relationships in the school. What does it mean for us to concern ourselves with thoughts of a spiritual nature about the evolving human being? It is a commitment to research and explore Steiner's thinking about the nature and development of the students who are placed in our care. Steiner was even more explicit about the importance of the teachers' meditative work in subsequent years. He was clearly expecting the teachers to take up what he was giving them not as mere information, but as themes for meditative contemplation. The Core Principles have been formed to support us in this work.

I experience the seventh principle addressing spiritual orientation as a remarkable invitation to become more authentically ourselves as individuals as we engage in becoming contemporary researchers of the path to incarnation of the human spirit. Each of us brings significant strengths as well as real challenges to our work. But we do not work in isolation. As Waldorf teachers and administrators, we have the remarkable opportunity—the responsibility, in fact—to share our work with one another, learning from the variety of approaches, successes, and failures that we experience. We have the responsibility to develop honest relationships among us, with all the difficulties that this can entail. We organize the daily life of running a school through shared agreements. All of this requires us to make commitments. These elements are part of the soul and spiritual architecture of our schools. These structures are the context for the students' experience of their education and will have a formative effect. As we live our commitments and agreements, day by day, we have the opportunity to model what it means to be in relationships that can develop. This process needs time— not too much, but enough. We can revisit our agreements when needed and exercise the kind of responsible innovation that requires dialog.

In an increasingly splintered and time-squeezed world, as described by some of our students, we can give them the soul space in which to breathe, and we can model for them an experience of relationship-building that the children and youth so sorely need. I often think about the freedom we have and wonder whether we are using that freedom to be as truly innovative as our times and the needs of our students are asking us to be. We have been given the gift of this work; what do we choose to do with it? And how do we shape it to meet the emerging future? It really is up to us.

Contributors

ADAM BLANNING, MD, practices Anthroposophic Medicine in Denver, Colorado. He works as a consultant (school doctor) for several Waldorf schools, actively lectures and writes on medicine and education, and directs the physician's training programs for Anthroposophic Medicine in the U.S. He is the author of *Seeing the Deeper Streams of Development*, due out laster this year.

DOUGLAS GERWIN attended Waldorf schools in Canada and the U.S. He has degrees in biology, psychology, and philosophy. He has been a Waldorf high school teacher and adult educator since 1983; Director of the Center for Anthroposophy (Wilton, NH) and Executive Director of the Research Institute for Waldorf Education (RIWE).

HOLLY KOTEEN-SOULÉ was a kindergarten teacher and parent/child leader for 25 years. She currently directs the Sound Circle Early Childhood In-Service Program in Seattle and Denver and serves as Chair of the WECAN Teacher Education Committee. She is also a member of the Pedagogical Section Council and the WECAN Board.

ELAN LEIBNER is certified in Waldorf education, remedial education, and Spacial Dynamics. He was a class teacher at the Waldorf School of Princeton for 18 years. He is an adult educator and mentor; chair of the Pedagogical Section Council of North America; and past editor of the *Research Bulletin* published by the Research Institute for Waldorf Education.

JUDY LUCAS is currently training in Rhythmical Massage Therapy as indicated by Ita Wegman, MD, and Margarethe Hauschska, MD. Before that she was the administrative director at the Denver Waldorf School for twelve years and also served as office manager, enrollment director and part-time high school language arts teacher. She received her Waldorf teacher training at Rudolf Steiner College. She serves on the Board of Trustees for the Association of Waldorf Schools of North America (AWSNA) and has served on the Pedagogical Section Council of the School for Spiritual Science since 2008.

JAMES PEWTHERER was the founding first grade teacher at the Hawthorne Valley Waldorf School, where he took two classes from grades 1–8 and then taught in the high school. He has served on the Pedagogical Section Council since its inception, for many years as its chair. He is also a member of the International Forum for Waldorf/Steiner Schools and participates actively in the work of AWSNA in many capacities.

JENNIFER SNYDER has been active in Waldorf education as a subject and class teacher, adult educator, and occasional lecturer in Northern California. She is a member of the Pedagogical Section Council, and she most recently founded and taught in a small, two-year Waldorf program for adolescents called Sungold Discovery Collaborative. Jennifer is currently enjoying mentoring class teachers in the Sacramento region.

FRANCES VIG, born and educated in England, is one of the founding members of the Chicago Waldorf School, where she has taken two classes from grade one through eight as well as being a subject teacher in the arts. She is currently a class advisor and high school teacher focusing on the sculptural arts and metalwork. A member of CWS's College of Teachers, Frances has worked in teacher development, served as College chair and as a member of the Board of Trustees. She also teaches in various anthroposophical conferences and adult training programs across North America, including the Arcturus Rudolf Steiner Education Program, of which she is a core faculty member. Frances is a member of the Pedagogical Section Council of North America, which she represents on the Leadership Council of AWSNA; she is also a member-at-large of the Teacher Education Network of AWSNA.

53118845R10071

Made in the USA
Middletown, DE
25 November 2017